WITHDRAWN

BIRDOLOGY

Young NATURALISTS

OTHER TITLES IN THE YOUNG NATURALISTS SERIES

Awesome Snake Science!
40 Activities for Learning About Snakes
by Cindy Blobaum

Insectigations
40 Hands-on Activities to Explore
the Insect World
by Cindy Blobaum

Birdology

30 Activities and Observations for Exploring the World of Birds

Monica Russo

Photographs by Kevin Byron

CHICAGO
REVIEW
PRESS

Published by Chicago Review Press Incorporated
814 North Franklin Street
Chicago, Illinois 60610
ISBN 978-1-61374-949-4

Library of Congress Cataloging-in-Publication Data
Russo, Monica, author.
 Birdology : 30 activities and observations for exploring the world of birds / Monica Russo ;
photographs by Kevin Byron. — First edition.
    pages cm
 Includes bibliographical references and index.
 ISBN 978-1-61374-949-4 (trade paper)
 1. Bird watching—Juvenile literature. 2. Bird attracting—Juvenile literature. I. Byron, Kevin,
illustrator. II. Title.

 QL676.2.R875 2015
 598.072'34—dc23

                         2014026071

Cover and interior design: Sarah Olson
Cover photos: Kevin Byron
Interior illustrations: Monica Russo
Interior photos: Kevin Byron

Printed in the United States of America
5 4 3 2 1

This book is dedicated to the "bird workers" across North America: bird banders, biologists, rehabilitation specialists and volunteers, conservationists, census workers, and bird-watchers observing as "citizen scientists"—all who help to study and define the range, home life, habitat needs, and population dynamics of birds.

The black-capped chickadee is the state bird of Maine and Massachusetts and the provincial species of New Brunswick, Canada.

Contents

Acknowledgments

This book would not have been possible without the help and generosity of many people. I would first like to express great appreciation of my parents, who were expert at creating gardens and habitats that attracted birds and other wildlife, for providing me with an early start in bird-watching and natural history experiences.

Kevin Byron's wonderful photographs in this book were taken over the course of many years, in a variety of habitats, and sometimes in very difficult conditions. This book, then, is also his, because the photos are vital to its design and presentation. Kevin was also our "systems manager," organizing the production details and communications.

Many thanks go to Dr. Heinz Meng, professor emeritus at SUNY in New Paltz, New York, for giving Kevin the opportunity over the years to observe and photograph peregrine falcons. Professor Meng pioneered the first captive-breeding programs to restore the peregrines. We also very much thank June Ficker, a federal bird bander at a local reserve, for providing much help and patiently letting us watch and photograph the banding process. The Center for Wildlife, a wildlife clinic and education center in southern Maine, was generous in allowing photos to be taken of birds in their care.

We hugely appreciated the exceptional garden sanctuary of our friends Dick and Jane, who are masters at creating varied habitats for birds and insect pollinators. And many thanks to my sister Sandy for reporting on birds seen to the south of us and making sure we had the equipment to create wonderful dinners to sustain us on this project! Thanks also go to Dean and Laura and Joyce, who alerted us to several photo ops. We also thank our friend Myra in Utah, who gave us the unique opportunity to observe and photograph the birds and plants of Park City.

Thanks and appreciation also go to Lisa Reardon, senior editor at Chicago Review Press, who guided us through the planning and development of this project.

Introduction

With the recent concern about possible "nature deficit" emerging in children and adults, there could be no better remedy than to experience the sights and sounds of the natural world.

Watching and listening to birds can provide feelings of personal discovery and accomplishment, and a rewarding outdoor experience. North America has more than 700 **species** of birds, and at least 9,000 are found around the world. You can find birds in the city and countryside, along the shore, and in forests, fields, and backyards. Birds are seen at zoos, museums, city parks, and even in our homes as pets. Birds appear on TV and in movies. They fascinate us with their variety of colors, patterns, songs, and activities, and they astonish us with their flight capabilities. Images and emblems of birds are historically important as icons of strength and freedom.

This book is not a field guide, so it does not focus on identifying species. Instead, the aim is to foster independent study through careful observation and hands-on activities. Parents, teachers, and students can easily participate in observing the birds around them: the variety of colors and patterns, the songs and calls, and the activities of feeding, preening (cleaning), or nesting. Even professional field biologists study birds simply by watching.

Although most of the birds in this book are wild **native species**, many **nonnatives** are included, such as the English sparrow, starling, and common pigeon. **Domesticated** birds such

Some of the species most familiar to us are pet birds and zoo birds. This is a male cockatiel. His name is Rocko.

as chickens, along with pet birds or birds seen in zoos and parks, are also included, because these birds are often the most familiar.

The time you spend watching birds now may lead to future study as a biologist, **ornithologist**, or bird **rehabilitator**—emerging on the forefront of new discoveries and adventures—to better understand the environment around us. And, studying birds is a lot of great outdoor fun!

A Note of Caution: Birds are protected by federal laws. It is illegal to collect any feathers, nests, or eggs of wild birds. These laws were made to prevent the kind of mass collection and destruction that caused the near **extinction** of some species in the 1880s.

It is *only* safe to observe, draw, or photograph any feathers found lying on the ground. They may have acquired harmful organisms that could cause infection if handled. The same caution must be used in studying hawk or owl **castings**: observe and record, but don't touch! These cautions are also explained in the text.

1

It's a Bird!

What makes a bird a bird? What makes birds special?
Birds are unique animals because they have feathers. But
feathers need a lot of care: preening and bathing are important.
Birds are fascinating to us because they make a huge variety of
sounds. It's fun to keep a bird journal so you can remember all the
sounds and songs you hear.

Feather Facts

Here are some basic facts about birds and their feathers:

- All birds have feathers—they are the *only* animals on earth that have feathers.

- Most birds can fly, but some can't. You probably already know that a penguin can't fly, and an ostrich can't fly, either. But they all have feathers.

- Feathers come in many shapes and sizes. A feather from a hummingbird is very small.

The Shapes of Feathers

Feathers may all appear to be the same shape, but they're not. See if you can notice the slight differences in the shapes of a variety of feathers.

Materials

- Just your eyes!

Birds "change their clothes" by **molting** (shedding) old feathers, usually in the fall, and sometimes again in the spring, so these are good times to do this activity.

Walk along a city sidewalk or hike in the woods and fields near your home. Look for feathers lying on the ground.

When you see a feather, observe its shape and try to determine what part of a bird it came from. A feather from a wing has a narrow vane on one side and a wider vane along the other side. It will also look stiff. Tail feathers are more flexible, and feathers from the center of the tail have an equal amount of vane on either side.

(right) This is a wing feather from a wild turkey and is about one foot (30.5 cm) long. The feathers on the wings and tails of most birds have a shape and design that helps them fly.

(left) Here is a tail feather from a blue jay.

The wing feathers on an eastern meadowlark in flight.

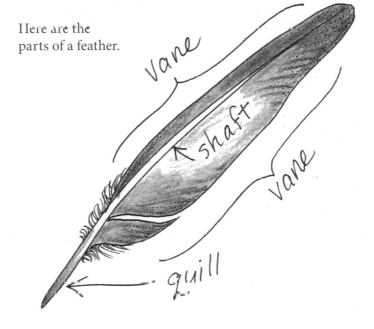

Here are the parts of a feather.

vane

shaft

vane

quill

How many feathers do you think are on one wing? A lot? There are usually 9 or 10 **primary** flight feathers—the pointier ones at the forward part of the wing—and 9 or 10 **secondary** flight feathers—the ones closer to the bird's body. If the bird has already molted a feather, there will be fewer. Birds drawn in cartoons or in animated movies often have too many wing feathers—or too few!

The small feathers covering the body of a bird—on its head and back, for example—are called contour feathers. The contour feathers of penguins are so narrow and fine that they look like fur!

Feathers on most newly hatched birds are very different than those on an adult. Whether you observe a fuzzy duckling on a farm or watch a television program showing bald eagle nestlings, these young birds will be covered in soft, fluffy down feathers.

Flight feathers on the wings enable birds to fly long distances, and some birds can fly very fast. The speed of a peregrine falcon can be about 200 miles per hour! But that's only when it is diving down onto its prey, with wings half-closed, in a plummet called a stoop. Most small birds easily fly at about 20 to 30 miles an hour for short distances.

A bird flying fast during **migration** may speed along at about 60 miles per hour.

Keeping Clean

All birds need to have clean feathers. Feathers have to be in perfect working order so a bird can fly. But feathers also keep a bird's body temperature just right, and they keep the bird dry. So birds frequently preen—that means a bird uses its beak to clean its feathers. It takes a feather in its beak and carefully pulls the length of the feather through to its end. A preening bird sometimes looks as if it is nibbling at its feathers.

This helps to clean dirt, dust, or mud from the feathers. It can also clean off tiny insect parasites such as lice. Another method of keeping clean is **anting**—settling down on or near an anthill. The bird spreads out its wings and tail, and as the ants crawl about they leave behind a substance (formic acid) that may repel parasites.

Birds also take baths to keep their feathers clean. A bird taking a bath in a puddle or a birdbath is very active, fluffing up its feathers, dipping its head in the water, and then shaking off the water with great energy.

Dust baths are also important to birds. Pigeons, doves, and English sparrows are

commonly seen fluffing their feathers and crouching down into fine sand to "dust" their feathers. Some researchers think this helps the birds to rid their feathers of parasites such as tiny lice or mites.

Birds also oil their feathers. Oil from glands at the base of the tail is picked up with the beak and rubbed across the feathers when the bird is preening.

Dinosaurs Had Feathers! Fossils of several different types of dinosaurs have been found that have clear impressions of feathers in the stone. *Microraptor*, *Anchiornis*, and *Confuciusornis* (kon-few-see-us-OR-nis) fossils, all found in China, are just

Here are the basic parts of a bird.

crown
nape
back
wing
rump
beak
breast
belly
thigh
tail
leg (Tarsus)
toes
claws (or talons, on a hawk or owl)

The flight feathers on the outspread wing of a peregrine falcon are easy to see.

Bird Words

- Birds belong to the class **Aves** (pronounced AY-veez). An aviary is a large cage for pet birds indoors or birds kept outdoors at a zoo.

- A scientist who studies birds is called an ornithologist (or-nih-THOL-oh-jist). An ornithologist might specialize in studying avian behavior, diseases, song patterns, or avian territories.

- A single type of bird is a species. (You can pronounce it either SPEE-seez or SPEE-sheez.) For example, there are many different species of sparrows; the song sparrow is just one species. The word is used whether you mean a single species or many different species—it is both singular and plural. There are over 700 species of birds in North America and at least 9,000 species around the world!

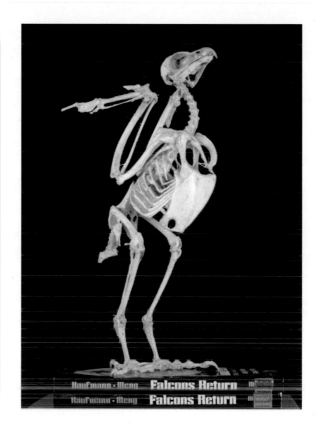

The large flight muscles lie against the protruding breastbone, or keel, seen here in the skeleton of a falcon.

a few of the birdlike dinosaurs that had feathers. All lived about 150 to 120 million years ago. *Confuciusornis*, only about one foot (30.5 cm) long, had long tail feathers. It may have been the first birdlike dino to have a true beak—with a point and no teeth. At least 500 fossil specimens of *Confuciusornis* have been found in China. It must have been fairly common. It is named after Confucius, an important Chinese philosopher who lived about 2,500 years ago.

It seems that each year, new fossils of feathered dinosaurs are discovered. Keep an eye out for news stories and science articles—you may read about a new finding yourself!

There are many kinds (species) of birds that *don't* fly. Here are a few:

- The kiwi of New Zealand. It just walks instead of flying. Its feathers look like fur.

- An ostrich. But it can *run* fast instead!

- Penguins. There are more than 12 species of penguins, and although they can't fly, they easily swim and dive in the ocean to catch fish. They kind of fly underwater.

- The rare kakapo, a type of parrot from New Zealand can only weakly glide, so it mostly walks everywhere.

A male yellow warbler.

Weird! Feathers are made of **keratin**, the same flexible protein that your hair and nails are composed of.

Anatomy

People who study birds also need to know the different parts of a bird. Anatomy is important when you need to describe the colors or patterns you see.

In addition to feathers, another **adaptation** for flight is a skeleton that is lightweight—some of the larger bones of a bird have air spaces inside, and the bones have thin walls.

Birds do not have teeth—or the heavier jaw needed to support teeth. Mergansers (diving ducks with narrow beaks) have serrated (saw-toothed) edges on their beaks. These serrations are not true teeth—just rows of tiny sharp points—but they help the mergansers catch and hold fish.

The front of a bird has to support big muscles for flying. These muscles lie against the protruding breastbone, or keel.

Name Game

You probably already know the different names for male and female chickens: a male is called a rooster or cock, and a female is a hen. A newly hatched chicken just out of the egg is called a chick. A female goose is—a goose! The males are called ganders, and the young ones are goslings.

Many other birds have different names for the males, females, and fledglings or hatchlings:

- A male swan is a cob.

- A female falcon is a falcon, but the male is a **tiercel** (TEER-sel).

- A male duck is called a drake.

- A young swan is a **cygnet** (SIG-net).

- A young hawk or falcon is an **eyass** (EYE-ess).

- A ruff is the name for a male sandpiper. Females are reeves.

- You might be surprised to find out that there is no such thing as a seagull. Although "seagull" is a commonly used name, you won't find it in any field guide or scientific book about birds. The correct name is simply "gull." But even a scientist will know what you mean.

- There are many species of sparrows. Many of them look alike, so they are very hard to identify and tell apart. There are many different species of warblers, also. Even an experienced

Songs, Calls, and Alarm Signals

With regular listening and observing, you can become an expert at figuring out which birds are making various noises, and why.

Materials

ʯ Your ears

ʯ Your eyes

Listen carefully. When you hear a bird making a noise, try to locate it and observe its markings and colors. Continue to listen while looking around you. Can you identify the conditions or circumstances that might be prompting it to speak up? A black-capped chickadee is named for its song of *chick-a-dee-dee-dee*. It also sings *chicka-chicka-dee-dee*. If it is alarmed by a nearby housecat, it usually calls out several *dee-dee-dee-dee-dee-dee* notes, to let other birds know of the terrible danger. Chickadees also have a call that sounds like *feee-bee*. Some birds have songs that are easy to remember, like the eastern towhee, which has a three-part song that sounds like *drink–your-TEA*. And it has a shorter call that goes *che WINK che WINK!* The beautiful yellow warbler has a rapid song that sounds like *sweet-sweet-sweet-it's-really-SWEET!*

bird-watcher might report that she or he saw "several warblers this morning" but was not able to identify them.

The groupings of different types of birds are listed at the end of this book. The scientific names for the species shown in this book are also listed.

Sounds Like a Bird!

Can you identify any bird songs yet? You may have already heard geese honking when they fly overhead or ducks quacking in a pond. Perhaps there are doves in your neighborhood that coo early in the morning. If you live near a farm or keep

A male grasshopper sparrow, singing.

chickens, you can easily tell the difference between a rooster crowing and chickens clucking.

The sounds from domesticated farmyard birds are good examples of the variety that a bird can make. If you visit a zoo, park, or nature center, you have an excellent opportunity to listen to different types of birds.

Pet birds such as parakeets, finches, or cockatiels also make songs, trills, and calls. Many pet parrots will even "comment" on household events, such as the entry of a person into the room.

If you can visit someone who has a pet bird, listen carefully to the whistles or calls it makes. Does it make different sounds if you open a door or if you drop something on the floor? Or if the owner offers it food? If someone runs a gush of water from the faucet, it may immediately make some excited sounds.

Some loud, hollow sounds are made by woodpeckers as they tap on rotting branches or dead trees, looking for beetle grubs (larvae) and other insects. The hairy woodpecker pecks rapidly on hollow branches to make a drumming noise. This probably lets other birds know that the tree is part of its **territory**. Both male and female hairy woodpeckers drum.

Hoot, Rattle, and Coo! Different species of birds can make an amazing variety of sounds: chipping, hooting, twittering, trilling, and sharp whistling. Some songs are very complicated, while some calls are simple loud honks, shrieks, or quacks. A belted kingfisher makes a sort of rattle as it flies out over a pond. The simple, harsh *caw* of a crow is easy to identify. The chipping sparrow has a steady sequence of *chip-chip-chip-chip* notes. A male grasshopper sparrow sings a song that is difficult to describe. It makes a few musical notes, followed by a series of rough buzzing sounds.

Don't Be Fooled!

Some species of birds are very good imitators—or mimics—of other types of birds. The blue jay is a good example. It can mimic the whistle of a red-tailed hawk or a red-shouldered hawk so well that even experienced bird-watchers look all around, expecting to see a hawk nearby. Jays can even mimic mechanical sounds. A blue jay with a territory near a car repair shop can imitate a power wrench!

Probably the best known mimic is the northern mockingbird. It learns to imitate the songs and sounds of other birds near its territory—even a rooster crowing. As it sings, you can hear a long sequence of several different songs and sounds. It may even imitate a creaky, rusty gate or a car alarm! Crows, starlings, catbirds, and brown thrashers are also good at mimicking and imitating.

Surprise! On a nature walk through a grove of pines, you might hear an excited chipping, chattering, and squealing. An intense search for a bird will be useless— because it is probably a red squirrel! Red squirrels make loud squeaks and chirrs that can easily be mistaken for a bird. They usually make these noises if another squirrel has invaded their territory.

A common mistake for beginning bird-watchers is to hear a soft cooing-hooing call and think it is an owl. But it usually turns out to be a mourning dove. Its call heard up close is a slow *coo-ahh, cooo-cooo-cooo*.

A red squirrel's chipping and chirping is sometimes mistaken for a bird's calls.

Start a Bird Journal

You can start your bird journal with some "Noise Notes." You've probably already heard quite a lot of different songs and calls by now. Keep a list of all the types of sounds you've heard, even if you don't know what species of bird made them. You're likely to find out later, through further observations.

Materials

- Notebook, 5 by 8 inches or 6 by 9 inches (12.7 by 20.2 cm or 15.2 by 22.9 cm)
- Ruler
- Pens or pencils

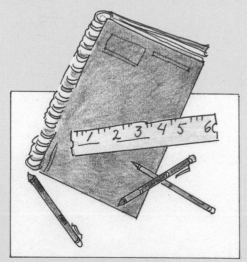

Your materials for starting a bird journal.

1. Use the ruler to mark off inches along one side of your notebook. This will help you to judge the length of any bird you might see singing and later help to identify the species.

2. When you hear a bird singing, write down where the song was heard, the date, and the time of day. Some birds, such as the white-throated sparrow, sing at dusk or at dawn.

3. Record why you think the bird was singing—was it announcing its territory or just twittering softly while at a bird feeder (something American goldfinches often do)?

   Your "Noise Notes" might look something like this:

March 19th
Heard a flock of geese honking as they flew overhead. It was so early, I was still in bed!

Later in town, there was a big flock of starlings making a lot of noise. Chattering, chirping, even buzzy sounds and squeals and whistles. They all sounded excited and happy.

At dusk—it was nearly dark!—there was a clear five-part song. The first note was a long whistle followed by four shorter notes that were higher. Maybe it was a white-throated sparrow?

4. Don't be afraid to write down any questions. You'll probably be able to answer them later. As the year goes by and you hear more and more bird "noise," you'll probably be able to identify the songsters.

2

Spots, Stripes, Dots, and Streaks

The colors and patterns on birds help us to identify the different species. Markings such as streaks, spots, and **wing bars** are usually easy to see. You may also notice a crest or the shape of a tail—and then start your own sketchbook of the designs and shapes you observe.

Field Marks

The patterns and designs on birds are called **field marks** because they are easy to see and remember "in the field"—while you are out walking or hiking in the woods, fields, or even in your own backyard. Some species of birds are named for their most obvious field marks: the black-capped chickadee has a distinct black "cap." The male red-winged blackbird has brilliant red "shoulders."

Many birds have rounded dots or spots on their breast or belly, such as the wood thrush. Many warblers, sparrows, hawks, and owls have streaks on their front feathers.

The killdeer is easily identified by two dark bands across its upper breast, while different species of plover at the shore have just one band.

There may also be a white or light-colored streak just above the eye, called an eyebrow. And others have a dark or light line that seems to go right across the eye—that's called an **eye-line** or **eye-stripe**.

Even the color of the eye is helpful when noting details of color and patterns. The common goldeneye duck has beautiful yellow-gold eyes. It also has a very obvious field mark: a large white spot on the side of its head.

The part of the eye that is colored is called the iris. (Humans usually have a blue or brown iris, but some people have greenish eyes, grayish eyes, or light brown "hazel" eyes.) The iris of most birds is dark brown. But many species, especially hawks, have eyes that are yellow for their first year and then gradually darken. The northern goshawk, Cooper's hawk, and sharp-shinned hawks all have yellow eyes when

(left) The red-breasted nuthatch has a long, black eye-line and a white line above it. This is a male.

(right) This close-up portrait of a Canada warbler clearly shows a distinct white eye-ring.

This common goldeneye duck has bright gold eyes and a telltale white spot on its face.

It's easy to identify a male common yellowthroat by its black "mask."

they are young. The iris becomes darker and darker until it is a beautiful red, like a garnet gemstone. It may take about three years for this to slowly happen.

The irises of a Brewer's blackbird are yellow. The eyes of a common loon are red. Most owls have yellow eyes, but the big barred owl and the ghostly pale barn owl both have dark brown eyes. However, when you see cartoons or animated movies of owls, the artists sometimes color the eyes bright yellow-gold (no matter what species it is) just so they look dramatic or frightening.

One forest bird is named for its beautiful eye color: the red-eyed vireo. It is fairly common in southern Canada and the

The cedar waxwing is light brown to caramel in color, with a small black mask across its eyes.

Field Marks

See if you can identify the field marks on a bird's wings, tail, and head.

Materials

↘ Just your eyes!

When you spot a bird, look for:

➤ Field marks on the wings: wing bars are thin white or light-colored "lines" across the upper wing.

➤ Field marks on the tail: a broad-winged hawk has bands of black and white across its tail. The tail of the eastern kingbird is tipped in white at the end.

➤ Field marks on the "face" and head: look at its eyes and beak. Many types of birds have a white eye-ring around the eye. This is easily seen on a Canada warbler (see previous page).

Start a Bird Sketchbook

Drawings and written observations are called field notes by naturalists and are very important in creating a good record of what you have seen and heard. Turn a small notebook with plain white pages into a bird sketchbook. Start by sketching field marks and interesting patterns.

Materials

- Scissors
- Piece of cardboard
- Notebook with plain white (unlined) pages
- Tape
- #2 pencil (or #3 pencil from an art store)
- Colored pencils, crayons, or felt-tipped pens

1. Cut the cardboard just slightly smaller than the size of your notebook and tape it to the back cover. This will give extra support while you are holding the sketchbook in your hand.

2. Use different pencils and pens for your drawings. The #3 pencil is softer than a #2, so it's a better choice if you want to shade in an area of a drawing. Or you might prefer colored pencils or felt-tipped pens. Try different types, and see which you like best.

3. Draw any interesting field marks, spots, or patterns you see. Don't worry that your drawings are not perfect—or even if they look cartoony. They are the notes you write down to help you remember what you've seen. As you make more and more drawings (and look at drawings other people have made of birds), you will start to develop an artistic eye for noticing designs and patterns on birds. It will help you later to identify the species and learn more about them.

(left) The male downy woodpecker has a small, squarish red patch on the back of its head.

(right) The male red-winged blackbird has bright red "shoulders."

eastern half of the United States, but it usually hunts for insects high in the trees—so you are not likely to see its eyes close-up.

Some birds, such as the male common yellowthroat, a warbler, have a "mask" across their face. (In older books, this small bird is called the Maryland yellowthroat. The common names of some species have changed over time, as researchers find out more about them.)

The cedar waxwing, a common songbird found across most of the United States and Canada, has a much smaller dark mask.

Different Designs

If you have ever seen a blue jay or a black-capped chickadee, you know that the males and females look alike. But for many other species, there's an obvious difference between the genders (sexes): the male red-winged blackbird has brilliant red "shoulders," but the female looks like a big brown-streaked sparrow.

A male northern cardinal is bright red, but the females are a dull reddish-tan. The male downy woodpecker and male hairy woodpecker both have a bright red patch on the backs of their heads, but the females have no red at all.

If you've ever looked at a flock of chickens, you can often tell the rooster (the male) from the hens (the females). The red comb on the head of a rooster is larger than a comb on a hen. The rooster is also larger and usually has longer, curved tail feathers.

But the gender difference is not as obvious for many wild species. Female American robins are somewhat paler or duller than the males. Female bluebirds are not as

Design-a-Bird

Design your own model bird! An easy way to remember and learn about different colors and patterns on birds is to create a "model" bird picture. You can make up any patterns and field marks and draw them on the outline.

Materials

- Tracing paper or access to a copy machine
- Colored pencils, crayons, or felt-tipped pens

1. Trace the outline of the bird shown here onto tracing paper (or make copies on a copier machine).

2. Draw in (on your tracing paper or copy) any field marks you want: an eye-ring, spots, streaks, or wing bars.

3. Draw in your choice for a tail shape, as shown: a forked tail, a square end, or a rounded end. You can add bands or bars across the tail.

4. Color in the bird with any colors or patterns you choose. Your "model bird" design will help you learn and remember field marks and different tail shapes when you see them.

forked   square   rounded

blue as their mates. And both robins and bluebirds have fledglings—young just out of the nest—that have spots all over their breast.

Some species have other colors or patterns that are easy to see and remember. The northern flicker, a woodpecker found over most of the United States and Canada, has a white rump. This is easy to spot when the bird takes off or is in flight. One small warbler is named just for its colorful rump: the yellow-rumped warbler, which can be distinguished from many other small birds by the yellow feathers at the base of the tail.

The brown thrasher, a large red-brown bird with a long tail found across much of eastern and central Canada and the States, has two thin white wing bars across its wings.

The northern mockingbird is gray, but it has large white wing patches that are easily noticeable as it flies or when it flashes open its wings.

(left) The yellow-rumped warbler is sometimes called the myrtle warbler in the eastern states.

(right) The brown thrasher has two white wing bars. It belongs to the same family as the mockingbird and has a variety of calls. Note the yellow iris.

The mockingbird flashes open its wings, showing the big white patches. It probably does this to warn other birds of its territory or preferred feeding area.

prismlike angles along the vanes of the feathers that strongly reflect blue light.

Can You See Me Now?

Many birds that look for food on the ground (or nest on the ground) have colors and patterns that blend in so well with the leaves around them that it is very hard to see them if they aren't moving. This **camouflage** is called **protective coloration**. A few good examples are the ruffed grouse, wild turkey, and woodcock. Whip-poor-wills and nighthawks also have great camouflage, which protects them at their nest on the ground.

Some birds are much lighter in color on their undersides. The eastern kingbird is mostly dark gray above, but its breast and belly are white. Tree swallows have white undersides. So do different species of chickadees, nuthatches, and several woodpeckers. This dark-above and light-below coloration is called **countershading** by biologists.

Many other animals have countershading, including red squirrels and gray squirrels, as well as some snakes, frogs, and toads.

Some of the colors of a bird's feathers are the result of substances called pigments, which may come from the food it eats. A male cardinal that eats mostly berries may look brighter red than a cardinal that eats mostly seeds. But other colors—such as the blue of a blue jay or an indigo bunting—are created by the structure of the feathers themselves. There are microscopic,

The barn swallow (*left*) has a very long forked tail. The tree swallow (*right*) has a shorter forked tail.

Tails to Tell

The tails of different species of birds end in different shapes, and in many cases, these shapes are a big help in identification. A goldfinch has a short tail that ends in a "notch" or V-shaped "fork." The barn swallow, common wherever there are open fields or meadows, has a very deep fork, with long feathers at each side. The tree swallow has a shorter, smaller forked tail.

If you live near the ocean or a large lake, you may have noticed the short, wide tails that gulls have. Many species of terns (which look like smaller, slimmer gulls) have somewhat forked tails.

3

Special Beaks and Feet

People have the ability to eat a variety of foods: fruits, vegetables, meats, eggs, cheeses, and breads. To eat these foods, we use knives, forks, and spoons. But a bird's "dinner utensils" are its own beak and feet. Some species eat mostly insects. Others eat mostly seeds. Herons and egrets eat mainly small fish. An owl hunts mice and other small rodents. Whether a bird eats seeds, insects, fish, or mice, it has adaptations that enable it to find, capture, and eat its meals.

A northern cardinal has a short but strong beak for opening hard seeds. This is a male.

Crunch and Munch

A lot of the birds we are familiar with are "seed eaters"—house sparrows, chipping sparrows, and goldfinches, for example. Larger species, including northern cardinals, evening grosbeaks, and rose-breasted grosbeaks, also eat seeds. Their beaks are short and are wedge-shaped or cone-shaped. They are very strong and can easily open up the different kinds of hulls and shells of seeds.

The cardinal eats many kinds of weed seeds and can easily crack open sunflower seeds one after another. But it also feeds on insects, including beetles and grasshoppers. It even eats spiders and slugs! But its big, strong beak is necessary to crack open the hard, frozen seeds that it finds during the winter.

Sparrows of many species generally eat seeds: tree sparrows, field sparrows, song sparrows, and white-throated sparrows, along with the chipping sparrows already mentioned. All these birds belong to the same family, and their beaks all have a similar shape. (The cardinal belongs to a different family, even though its beak looks the same.)

Finches are members of yet another group, a family that includes the goldfinch, house finch, and purple finch—and all have seed-eating beaks like sparrows.

Most of the seed-eaters also eat other foods, especially during the warmer months. An evening grosbeak will eat beetles, spiders, and moth larvae (caterpillars). A cardinal will feed on the berries of some shrubs. A purple finch might eat juniper berries if they are abundant.

Other birds that don't have short, conical beaks eat seeds, too. City pigeons (rock doves) will flock to seed set out on the ground for them in parks and backyards.

You can do an experiment to see what birds in your neighborhood are attracted to seeds. A variety of seeds is available for feeding wild birds: millet, niger (thistle), striped sunflower seed, black oil sunflower seed, and safflower, just to name a few. If you buy a bag of "mixed seed," read the ingredients, so you know what seeds are in the mix. (If the main ingredient is corn, you will probably attract mostly squirrels!)

Tap Tap Tap

Woodpeckers have beaks that are somewhat long and narrow. But they are very strong beaks, because they tap and peck into rotting tree trunks, fallen logs, and thick branches. Woodpeckers use their beaks to push off and lever away flakes of bark and old decaying wood from trees, stumps, and logs. Rotting trees and stumps are the places where the larvae (grubs) of beetles live, and they are the food of choice for woodpeckers.

A woodpecker's specialized beak is also used for communication. By tapping very rapidly on a hollow tree trunk or branch, a woodpecker can make a drumming sound that can easily be heard by any other bird—or person—in the vicinity.

Hairy woodpeckers are common in woodlands across most of the United States—even Alaska—and much of Canada. Both males and females rapidly "drum" or "drill" on trees in the spring to let other birds know that the trees are part of their territory.

There are several species of woodpeckers across North America, so your chances of seeing one or hearing one are quite good. One species, the northern flicker, frequently feeds on the ground, often on a sunny lawn, pecking into the dirt for ants.

TRY THIS!

Feed the Birds

Find out what kind of seeds attract the birds in your backyard or neighborhood.

Materials

✎ A small bag of "wild birdseed" (available at grocery or pet supply stores)

1. Read the ingredients on the birdseed bag, so you know what type of seeds are included

2. Sprinkle the seed around in different places: a grassy area, the edge of a lawn, near a shrub, or under a tree. Don't place seed near a road or along a driveway.

3. Watch from a window or even sit on a chair or bench outside, just as long as you are well away from the seeds. Be patient. If you have never fed birds in that area, it could be hours—or days!—before they come down to feed.

Even if you are not able to set out seed for this experiment yourself, you might find out if there is a nearby sanctuary, nature center, or park where birds are fed. Ask what type of seed is used and what birds are "regular customers."

The hairy woodpecker has a beak that it uses to peck and tap into decaying logs and branches to find beetle grubs. This is a female.

The largest woodpecker in North America is the pileated (PY-lee-ay-tid), about the size of a crow, with a bright red crest. Like other woodpeckers, it hunts for ants, beetles, and larvae in dead trees, stumps, and branches by pecking the wood apart with its beak. Some of the holes it makes are square-shaped openings that almost look like small doorways hacked into the tree. Those shapes are a hallmark of a pileated woodpecker's work. You will also find large splinters and pieces of rotting wood at the base of the tree or stump that the bird had been pecking at. The pileated and other woodpeckers use their beaks like a chisel to break away flakes of bark and pieces of wood.

Woodpeckers also need to tap and chisel and hack away the old dead wood to make their nests. They may look for a rotting tree that already has a hole in it, and then they enlarge the hole and chisel out the inside of the tree, excavating enough material to make it big enough for a nest.

Beaks Up Close

If you or anyone in your family has a parakeet or cockatiel, you know firsthand that the beak looks strong and has an impressive curved point. That's because these birds can eat a variety of foods. They eat mostly seeds, but in the wild they also eat fruit and some insects. Pet birds in the parrot family may include the parakeet, cockatiel, "love birds," and different types of conures. (Parakeets are often called budgies

(left) A parakeet has a curved beak. At the top of the beak, notice the blue cere (the bulge where the nostrils open). This is a male. Females have a light brown cere.

(right) A great blue heron waits patiently in the tall grasses of a marsh for prey to appear.

Walk Like a Heron

How do the size of your feet and the length of your stride compare to those of a heron?

Materials

- Scissors
- Measuring tape
- Roll of brown kraft paper or the white side of a roll of wrapping paper
- Tape
- Colored pencils, crayons, or felt-tipped pens
- A helper

1. Cut a length of paper about 6 feet (1.83 m) long and tape it to the floor to keep it in place.

2. Draw the tracks of a heron along one side of the paper. (Use the track in the drawing as your model.) Each track has three forward toes and one hind toe and is just more than six inches (15.2 cm) long, with about nine inches (22.9 cm) between tracks.

3. Now have a helper draw the outline of your shoe, as you take each step walking next to the heron tracks. You will probably be able to take four steps. Look at the tracks of your shoes next to the heron's tracks and compare how you walked. Did you take the same number of steps? Your shoes are probably longer than the heron's foot, but you might find that the distance between each step is the same!

Imagine walking quietly along the edge of a big pond or lake and looking down into the water for fish. You would need to take careful steps so you don't frighten away any prey, and then you would need a big spearlike beak to quickly jab down to catch it! Your long toes help you to stand motionless and steady in the soft mud as you wait for prey.

Can I go fishing now!

A northern goshawk has a sharp beak for ripping apart the meat and tendons of its prey. The eyes of this "gos" still have a yellow iris, which means it is about one year old. An older goshawk would have red eyes, and its feathers would be silver-gray, instead of brown.

in England and Australia. It's a short name for the native Australian word budgerigar [BUD-jeer-ih-gar]).

Pet parrots of all kinds are often fed only seeds, but they may also need other types of food to be healthy. It's best to read about the species of pet bird you have to understand its food requirements. Watch closely while a parrot or parakeet eats to see how it uses it beak. Larger parrots sometimes use their feet to hold onto food.

Beaks Like a Spear

Herons and egrets all have long legs, long necks, and long, strong beaks. They are all "wading birds," carefully stepping into the water of lakes, ponds, and ocean inlets or estuaries to hunt for fish or frogs. They need long legs to wade in as deep as they can and very long toes, which help to support them in mud or soft sand. Their beaks are long and sharp, like fishing spears, which they quickly jab into the water whenever they see a fish or other prey.

The toes of a great blue heron are long. Each separate footprint or track a heron leaves in the sand is just more than six inches (15.2 cm) long! How long are the shoes you are wearing?

Raptor Beaks

Birds of prey such as hawks, falcons, eagles, vultures, and owls are also commonly called raptors, although they belong to different families. They all have beaks that are curved, with a very sharp point at the tip. Most birds of prey hunt, catch, and kill their own food. A few, like the turkey vulture, feed mostly on **carrion** (dead animals). A vulture may also feed on the "leftovers" from an animal that another raptor has killed or on the carcass that a wolf or other large predator has left. It may even eat from a road-killed animal.

When a hawk kills its prey—or a vulture eats from the leftovers of a wolf's dinner—it needs a sharp, hooked beak to rip apart its food. An animal's muscle and fat is not too difficult for a hawk or falcon to rip apart, but it may even have to rip smaller bones right out of their sockets. That's a lot of work to get your dinner, so a sharp beak is necessary.

Even small hawks and falcons have sharp beaks for tearing up meat. The American kestrel hunts mostly grasshoppers and mice, but its beak is the same shape as a larger falcon. And the tiny falconets (species from Borneo, Sumatra, and the Philippines) have similar beaks—even though the falconets are only the size of a house sparrow—about six inches (15.2 cm) long!

Just Poking Around

Birds that probe down into mud or loose soil for their food have long, thin beaks. In dry woodlands, the American woodcock is a good example, because it hunts for worms and small insects just under the thick layers of dead leaves. The flightless kiwi of New Zealand also uses its long beak to find food, poking its beak into the ground searching for insects and worms.

If you live near the shore or visit the coast for a summer vacation, you're likely to see a variety of shorebirds that also use their beaks for poking and probing. Willets, yellowlegs, whimbrels, and dowitchers all look for food near the water. Sandpipers and plovers hunt at the water's edge or poke and probe in the tide line of sea wrack—the messy accumulation of seaweed, shells, and sea urchins or starfish left on shore by the last high tide.

Beaks for Bugs

Some of the smallest and narrowest beaks are those of the insect-eating birds. They have to be able to pick out and capture small insects from leaves and twigs. Warblers and vireos have beaks that enable them to pick up very small insects, such as aphids—tiny bugs often found in gardens and on shrubs. Flycatchers and swallows have small beaks, too, but they usually catch their prey "on the wing," in midair while they are flying. Imagine trying to catch a mosquito while it is flying by—with just a small beak! Most insect-hunting birds also have toes that can grasp strongly onto small branches while they climb and hop through the trees looking for food.

Web Masters

It may seem that a bird's wings are the most important part of its body, enabling it to get where it needs to go. But for ducks, geese, swans, and other birds, feet are just as important. Ducks need to swim, and their big, webbed feet are perfect adaptations for paddling around a quiet pond or lake. But some species need to dive deep to find their food. Canvasbacks, redheads, greater scaup, surf scoters, common goldeneyes, and several other species are all called diving

This beautiful prairie warbler feeds mostly on insects. It has a small beak for picking up tiny prey and has toes that firmly grasp onto small twigs while it hunts.

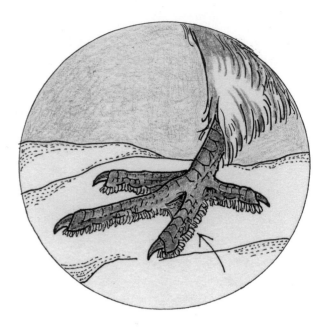

(left) Ducks need big, wide, webbed feet to swim. This is an American black duck.

(right) The ruffed grouse has tiny scalelike ridges along each toe that help it to walk and run across snow and ice.

ducks because they dive down to find and catch their food underwater.

Other types of swimming and diving birds include loons and mergansers. Grebes have flat lobes on each toe, so each toe is like a narrow paddle. And of course, penguins have webbed feet.

Winter Snowshoes

In northern areas and up into the Arctic, some birds have to walk across the snow and ice. Ruffed grouse have tiny, tough projections along the side of each toe, like narrow scales, that help them to walk steadily on the snow. And ptarmigans

(TARM-ih-gans), similar to grouse, have feathered toes that help give them steady footing in the snow. Ptarmigans also molt their brown summer feathers to acquire white ones as camouflage for the winter months.

These Feet Were Made for Walking (and Running and Hopping)

Members of the thrush family, which includes the American robin, hermit thrush, and wood thrush, among others, are species that spend much of their food-searching time walking on the ground.

You might not get a good chance to closely watch forest thrushes like the wood thrush, but you should be able to observe the American robin while it hunts on a lawn, a playground, or in a park for food.

Many other birds need to walk around on the ground to find tiny prey such as insects, worms, millipedes, sowbugs, or spiders. One of the most interesting is the ovenbird, found in woodlands and forests across much of the United States and southern Canada. The ovenbird is named for the structure of its nest, which is placed on the ground and covered partly over with an arch of leaves, like an old-fashioned brick oven. Its song is a loud, memorable

Hopping or Walking

Keep an eye on a robin for different types of walking and hopping when it hunts.

Materials

🔧 Just your eyes!

Refer to the picture of a robin at right. When you spot a robin outdoors, notice that it might:

➤ Run and stop, run and stop.

➤ Hop and stop.

➤ Tilt its head and look down, each time it stops.

A robin usually moves ahead in short bursts—either hopping, walking, or running—and then stops to see if there is any prey, tilting its head. Watch to see if the

robin pulls an entire worm up out of the ground, a small grub, or some crawling insect.

Note: the American robin is not the same as the English robin, which is often seen on Christmas cards. It is a completely different species!

An American robin hunts for food on a grassy lawn.

"TEA-cher, TEA-cher, TEA-cher," repeated rapidly.

When the ovenbird walks, it steps carefully along, almost as if its feet hurt a lot or as if it were walking on the moon. It is a funny sight to see. It doesn't usually hop along. You might think something was wrong with its feet, but that's just the way it moves, sneaking quietly over the dead leaves and pine needles on the ground.

An ovenbird walks along carefully and quietly. It steps cautiously, as if sneaking up on an insect.

Claws for Clinging and Grabbing

Woodpeckers have feet and claws that are perfect for climbing up and down on tree trunks and branches. Some tree trunks have rough bark that is easy to cling to, but other trees have smooth bark that is more difficult to climb around on.

There are two forward-facing toes on most woodpeckers and one or two backward-facing toes. This arrangement helps them to cling and climb, whether they are going up a tree or downward. Most birds have four toes—three forward toes and one hind toe. But some shorebirds have only three toes while others have a hind toe reduced in size, so it is very small. The ostrich has only two toes, but they are very large and sturdy.

Nuthatches also have claws adapted for climbing on tree trunks and branches. The white-breasted nuthatch is fairly common throughout most of the United States and southern Canada. It is often mistaken for a woodpecker because it has a similar beak and can climb up and down the trees easily. But it belongs to a different family.

Not Just Claws—Talons!

Most birds of prey, or raptors, have the large claws needed for grasping their food. The claws are called talons. Large owls, hawks, falcons, and eagles have large talons, of course. But even smaller raptors, such as the American kestrel and the sparrow-sized falconets of Southeast Asia, have sharp, curved talons to catch and grasp their prey and rip the meat apart.

(left) The feet of a woodpecker have curved claws, which they need to cling to tree trunks.

(right) The legs and toes of the snowy owl are covered in small feathers. It has large, curved talons. This owl was injured and lives at a wildlife rehabilitation center.

The feet and talons of a peregrine falcon are adaptations for capturing their prey. This is a trained falconer's bird.

The snowy owl is a large predator that lives on the arctic **tundra**, where snow and ice cover the ground during much of the year. The legs and toes of the snowy owl are covered in small feathers, and it has large talons for capturing and grasping its prey. This owl is the official bird of the province of Quebec, Canada. It is sometimes seen in the northern United States when severe winter weather drives it southward to look for food.

The large feet and talons of a peregrine falcon are quite impressive. These raptors sometimes hunt for prey as large as ducks. They need to have long, strong toes and curved talons—and a sharp beak capable of capturing and killing their prey swiftly and then ripping apart meat, tough tendons, and cartilage.

The American bald eagle has very strong toes and large talons and usually feeds on fish. So does the osprey, an eagle-like raptor that nests in Canada, the United States, Great Britain, and Scandinavia.

Amazing Wings and Eyes and Notable Nests

Birds around the world have special adaptations to fly, to hunt for food, and to build their nests. Their wings, eyesight, and ability to collect nesting material—even mud—are truly amazing.

(left) The wingspan of a great egret is about 50 inches (127 cm) across.

(right) The wings of a pigeon make an obvious noise or "clap" when it takes off from the ground.

Wings of All Sizes

You don't have to be good at math or memorizing numbers to be amazed and impressed by these facts about birds' wings.

- The wingspan of most hummingbirds is only three to four inches (7.6 to 10.1 cm) across.

- The wingspan of a great egret is 50 inches (127 cm) across.

- The wingspan of a great horned owl is about 44 inches (111.7 cm) wide.

- The wingspan of a red shouldered hawk is about 40 inches (101.6 cm) across.

- The wandering albatross has a wingspan of 11½ feet (3.5 m).

- The Marabou stork has a wingspan of 12 feet (3.6 m) across! Wow!

Wing Fling. Hummingbirds get their name from the whirring, humming noise their wings make. But the wings of other birds make different sounds. If you hear a flock of geese or ducks take off from the ground, you can easily hear their wings flap. But you would probably not be able to hear an owl fly by—even a large owl. The wing feathers of an owl have a soft, velvety surface, which keeps the wings from

Measure Your Wingspan

How does your "wingspan" compare with that of some of the big birds?

Materials

- Piece of light-colored string about 12 feet (3.6 m) long (That's the wingspan of a Marabou stork—imagine having wings like that!)
- A friend
- Ruler, yardstick, or measuring tape
- Roll of brown kraft paper or the white side of a roll of wrapping paper
- Crayons

1. Use the string to measure your own "wingspan." With one hand, hold onto the end of the string at your fingertips.

2. Grab the string with the fingertips of your other hand. Stretch out your arms, holding the string tightly. Have a friend mark the length of the string between your fingertips with a crayon.

3. Put the string on the floor or ground, stretch it out, and measure the length of string from its end to the crayon mark. This would be your wingspan, if you were a bird. Now you can make a drawing of your own "wings."

4. Spread out the roll of kraft paper and use the yardstick or measuring tape to mark the endpoints of your wingspan based on the measurement you just took.

5. Draw in feathers where your fingertips would be, and draw the rest of the wings toward the center, where a bird's body would be. Do you have the wingspan of a golden eagle? Probably not—it's about 78 inches (198 cm) across! Or the wingspan of a raven? That would be about 53 inches (134.6 cm). You might have a wingspan greater than a snowy egret—just more than 40 inches (101.6 cm) across.

The "Clap" of Wings

Do birds clap their wings? Listen hard and find out.

Materials

↘ Your eyes

↘ Your ears

Stand and watch a flock of rock doves (pigeons). When they take flight, listen for the "clap" of their wings. Compare that sound with the flight of other birds. A hummingbird's flight is just a quiet hum. Ducks and geese are much louder. And chickens often stand still and flap their wings loudly, even if they don't fly away.

A pileated woodpecker can see a grub close-up and then see far away to the next branch it will fly to. This is a male pileated.

making very much noise. That's a big help when silently hunting mice at night.

Some birds, such as doves, quail, and grouse, have stiff, slightly curved wing feathers. When these birds fly, the wings make a whirring noise. People hiking or hunting are often quite startled when a covey (group) of quail suddenly bursts into flight just ahead of them!

Amazing Eyes

When a Cooper's hawk flies through the forest, it zips speedily past all the branches. Imagine if you could run through a forest as fast as you could possibly go, without running into a tree trunk or a branch! The hawk can see far ahead and not run into anything. Imagine being a red-tailed hawk soaring high above a field and then suddenly zooming down to catch a small mouse. If you were a flycatcher, you could quickly dart out from your perch and snap up a tiny fly that was many yards away.

Birds need very good vision to be able to get their food and to keep a lookout for predators. Most birds see in color just as you do, but they also have the ability to adjust their vision much better than we can. They can see things that are close-up or far away in sharp detail, better than humans. This is called accommodation. They can focus on something tiny or far away and see it clearly and then focus on something close-up. Having good accommodation is necessary to hunt for tiny insects or find a small mouse in a large field and then fly off to a perch far away.

That's Weird. If you face forward and don't move your head, you can still move your eyes all the way to the left or right. An owl cannot move its eyes to the left or right like you can—but it can turn its head around to look "over its shoulder" instead. However, an owl *cannot* turn its head all the way around in a full circle, the way birds in cartoons do!

Ultraviolet Light. Most birds see their world in color, just as you do. But many species also see **ultraviolet light**—UV for short. UV is a type of light that humans can't see. It is near violet on the visible spectrum of light—but we can't see it. Many flowers have patterns and designs colored in ultraviolet light, which insects can see. And some birds have feathers with UV patterns.

Most birds have excellent color vision. However, biologists are finding that owls have poor color vision—and perhaps see only black and white. Most species of owls are nocturnal (active at night) and use their good hearing, along with sharp vision, to

find their prey. They are instantly alert if they hear a mouse squeak or if there is a rustle in the leaves below.

Notable Nests

The nests of eagles and ospreys are among the largest of any species. The nest of an osprey is often five to six feet (1.5 to 1.8 m) across. They use large branches and sticks, of course, but ospreys add other items to

A great horned owl has excellent vision and easily hunts its prey at night.

 **LOOK FOR**

Eyes, Right!— and Left

The eyes of an owl are on the front of its head—just like yours. But there's one big difference. Pretend to be an owl and learn what it is.

Materials

✄ Just your eyes!

Stand still, face forward, and move your eyes all the way to the right without moving your head. Now look all the way to the left. An owl cannot do this. Because it can't move its eyes, it has to turn its head from side to side. Imagine that you are an owl and must turn your head to look at anything. If you try doing this, it kind of feels like you're a robot, doesn't it?

Hummingbirds use lichens (left) and moss (right) in nest construction.

This osprey nest is built about 25 feet from the ground, on a platform set up just for their use. The parents were successful, raising three youngsters.

the nest material. The list of strange items includes seaweed, shells, and even long pieces of bright orange plastic rope! A nest may be reused for several years, with more sticks and odd materials added over time.

The smallest nests are those of hummingbirds—only two inches (5 cm) across! Hummingbirds use lichens and moss to build their nests, which help to camouflage them completely. Spiderwebs are also used in nest construction, along with the fuzzy covering of "fiddle-heads" (the curled fronds of ferns just before they spread open).

Most small birds such as warblers, vireos, sparrows, and finches nest in trees using twigs, grasses, and plant stems as building materials. Chickadees, nuthatches, and woodpeckers look for an old decaying tree that they can peck into and excavate a nest cavity. They carry beakful after beakful of rotten wood or splinters from the inside, making it large enough for a

nest. They may also modify a nest that another bird used during the previous year. A wooden birdhouse may also be used, especially if the entrance hole is not bigger than 1¼ inch (3.2 cm) in diameter.

Wrens are well known for making more than one nest but using only one. Male wrens often build as many as four or five extra nests, and then only one is used to raise a family. They are also known for adding odd materials, including pieces of metal such as nails and paper clips.

Orioles build basketlike nests, hung from the ends of branches. The nests look unsafe to a human—imagine being in a woven basket or pouch, high up in a tree, dangling from the branches! But the nest is strongly woven, built from grasses and strands of bark from grapevines. The orioles won't use the same nest the following year, but if they were successful, they may build again in the same tree or in another nearby.

Home Decorating? Ospreys and wrens are not the only birds to add odd things to their nests or nest sites. In Australia, the bowerbirds are famous for collecting odd objects to place around their nest. One species looks for green objects, and another chooses to collect blue items. They may pick up colored stones, shells, flowers, feathers, and even pieces of glass.

On the Floor and in the Dirt. Several species of forest birds don't nest in trees at all but nest on the forest floor (on the ground). Their nests are camouflaged by fallen leaves, twigs, ferns, and moss. A few of these species include the veery, hermit thrush, ovenbird, and the black-and-white warbler.

Some birds make their nests underground or in tunnels. In the United States and Canada, the belted kingfisher makes a tunnel in the dirt of a sandbank or bluff near a pond or lake. In Florida, burrowing owls nest in burrows that they dig into soft, sandy areas.

Perhaps the strangest nest is that of the Australian malleefowl. The male scrapes and scratches together a pile of dirt—a big pile, about five feet (1.5 m) high! The female digs into it to lay about 20 to 25 eggs, and the male guards the huge pile of dirt, which is warmed by the sun, until the eggs hatch.

This robin's nest was built only a few feet from the deck of an apartment building.

 TRY THIS!

Help Birds Build Their Nests

Hang out nesting material in the spring for birds.

Materials

- Scissors
- Thick string (not sewing thread), yarn, twine, or thin strips of cloth (choose materials that have natural colors)
- Your bird journal

1. Cut the string, yarn, twine, or cloth strips into 10 to 20 pieces of about five inches (12.7 cm) long each.

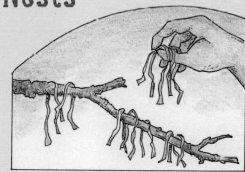

2. Hang the pieces of string and other material on a branch, railing, or fence where birds can easily see them and pick them up. Do not use thin sewing thread or pieces longer than five inches, because it could cause a tragedy—the birds may get tangled up in longer pieces and choke, or the nestlings may strangle in long, loose pieces. Don't use brightly colored string, because that may attract the notice of predators.

3. Watch for birds coming to look at the nesting material. Which kind of twine or yarn do they choose? Do they take more than one piece at a time?

4. Write down what you find out in your bird journal so that you know what the best materials are for next time.

No Nest at All! There are two birds famous for not making any nest at all. One is the brown-headed cowbird, found in much of Canada and across the United States. The female visits another bird's nest just long enough to lay her egg in it, and then she flies away. She'll often choose the nest of a yellow warbler or song sparrow. Sometimes the owner of the nest is aware of what has happened, and the cowbird's egg is shoved out of the nest. But often the cowbird egg hatches, and the nestling is fed and cared for by the foster female, along with her own nestlings. Even though the cowbird chick is much bigger than her own chicks, it still gets fed!

Cuckoos are also famous for not making a nest, but there are several species of cuckoos. The two species in the United States and Canada make their own nests. But the common cuckoo of England, Europe, Scandinavia, Africa, and Asia is a different species, and it lays its eggs in the nests of other birds.

Just Ducky. The hooded merganser, a duck that is found in much of Canada and the United States, builds its own nest, but the female will sometimes lay eggs in the

(left) A nest of barn swallows on the rafters of an open storage shed.

(right) A cliff swallow nest under the eaves of a house in Maine. The mud was collected from a pond at a nearby golf course.

nest of another duck, the common goldeneye. The goldeneye will raise the merganser's chicks with her own. The females of both these species lay 10 to 12 eggs each. Wood ducks, mallard ducks, and gadwall ducks also lay about the same number of eggs.

Some species don't make much of a nest at all. Many terns and plovers nest right on the sand at undisturbed or protected beaches. Their eggs are usually laid in a shallow depression in the sand, but they don't make a real nest. Sometimes the female may add a bit of seaweed or a few shells, but usually the nest site is quite bare.

Around the House. Robins often build their nests close to a house, especially in evergreens such as hemlocks or arborvitae (ar-bor-VY-tee). They build a neat, cup-shaped nest of weed stems, fine twigs, and rootlets, and then add a lining of mud. Then they finish the inside with softer, fine grasses, string, or strips of cloth. The female usually lays four or five eggs.

In and out of the Barn. An open barn, garage, or large, open garden shed is likely to attract barn swallows, which tuck their nests onto the rafters. The swallows have to be able to come and go freely, flying in and out of the open doors all summer or through windows left open during the nesting season. The nests are constructed of mud, straw, and grasses or stems. The mud is brought in by the beakful—the swallows have to make many trips out to the edge of a pond to scoop up mud or clay! The nest is lined with fine grasses and maybe even chicken feathers collected from a nearby barnyard.

Barn swallows are found in Canada, the United States, England, Europe, Asia, and Africa. They have even been reported as **accidentals** in Australia! They are desirable and beneficial birds, because they eat small insects such as mosquitoes and flies. They catch them on the wing, snapping them up as they fly back and forth over fields.

Like barn swallows, cliff swallows also nest under roof eaves. They are found across Canada and the United States, even north to Alaska. They also nest under the overhangs of sheds, on rocky cliffs, or under bridges. Cliff swallows build gourd-shaped or bottle-shaped nests made entirely of mud, using only a bit of fine grass for a lining. Like other species of swallows, cliff swallows feed on flying insects.

5

Birds Are Everywhere

Birds are found almost everywhere: from the freezing cold tundra of the Arctic where snowy owls and gyrfalcons live to hot rain forests to dry sagebrush deserts. In Antarctica, there are colonies of penguins. But you don't have to go that far to see interesting birds. There are plenty of birds to observe all around you, even in the largest cities in the world.

City Streets and Local Parks

You've probably already seen common pigeons on city streets or in parks. Naturalists and ornithologists call them rock doves. Rock doves can be seen on sidewalks looking for bread crumbs and insects and will get very close to people who are feeding them. They are so common that if you watch a television program about a foreign city halfway around the world, you are likely to see them in the background!

Also called rock pigeons, they are not a species native to North America. That means that they were never found there in the wild but were brought there instead. Rock doves are native and wild in Europe, but in the early 1600s, they were brought to the American colonies. They adapted very well to their new surroundings and are now found across the United States and southern Canada. In their native European **habitat**, they nest on cliffs and rocky ledges near the sea. In North America, they may

nest on the ledge of a large building, the supports under a bridge, or on the rafters of a barn.

Whether you call them pigeons or rock doves, they are a fascinating part of human history because they have been raised in captivity by people for hundreds of years. Careful breeding of rock doves has resulted in many different varieties. Some of these have curly feathers on the neck, feathered legs, white feathers, or the ability to fly in a sort of "tumble."

Another variety is the racing pigeon, raised for speed. Also called homing pigeons, they are kept in flocks in small houses called dovecotes or pigeon lofts. They can be released far from their homes and will return directly back to their own dovecote. Homing pigeons have also been used to carry messages written on small pieces of paper. The slips of paper are rolled up and put into tiny capsules on bands on the birds' legs. When the "carrier pigeon" returns to its home loft or cote, the message is taken out and read.

Pigeon Perfect? Rock doves (common pigeons) all seem to look the same. They are gray, with two darker bands across the wings and a wide, dark band across the end of the tail. But there are almost always some color or pattern variations. If you see

Look for variations among birds in a flock of rock doves. This one has white wing feathers instead of gray.

Pigeon Particulars

If you have a flock of rock doves in your area that you can observe, look for these behaviors:

- Drinking water. Pigeons drink differently from many other birds. They seem to suck the water in instead of dipping their beaks in and lifting their heads up.
- Following and chasing each other. Males can be aggressive, rushing at other males to keep them away from a feeding spot. Males may also run after females in the hope of finding a mate.
- Puffing and strutting. Males have glossy, iridescent necks (their feathers reflect light), and they puff up their neck feathers and strut around to impress a female.
- Preening. Pigeons preen frequently. Watch to see what feathers they start with.

A male house sparrow surveys his territory from a fence post.

a flock of rock doves in a park or on a city sidewalk, take the time to look at each one. Within a large group, there are likely to be a few individuals that have different colors or patterns. One may have brown feathers or be darker gray than the others. Another may have spots or patches of white. One may even have white wings.

Not Just Pigeons

Another common bird on city streets and in parks is the house sparrow, also called the English sparrow. This bird is native to Great Britain, Europe, Africa, and Asia. Wild-caught house sparrows were brought to the New York City area in the early 1850s. Since then, they have adapted to their new environment, increased in numbers, and spread across most of North America.

Whether you call them house sparrows or English sparrows, you are most likely to see them in towns and cities or near farms and parks. They are often seen on the ground at the edge of parking lots or on sidewalks, foraging for food in the discarded litter and food wrappers that people carelessly throw out.

House sparrows sometimes take over the nesting sites of native wild birds. They have become a considerable problem in some areas where nesting boxes for bluebirds, martins, or tree swallows are set out. They have been known to invade a nest box, and if the bluebirds don't leave, the house sparrows will make a nest right on top of

A flock of starlings perched on telephone lines is a common sight in many cities.

and land together where there is food. They will even hop around under cars in a parking lot, looking for crumbs. And they may retreat in a small group to a hedge or evergreen tree where they can watch out for food. You may also see two house sparrows fighting intensely—they will fly at each other and come to the ground with one grasping the other's leg with its beak!

Another common nonnative species is the starling, brought to the New York City area around 1890. It successfully adapted to its new environment and now nests across all of the United States and much of Canada. Starlings seem to nest everywhere in cities and towns. They gather in large flocks in the spring and fall, and many people think they are noisy nuisances. They are frequently seen on lawns, eating grubs and worms. Starlings are often called blackbirds, but they are not related to our native red-winged blackbird, rusty blackbird, or Brewer's blackbird. In fact, starlings belong to the same family as the mynah bird of China and Southeast Asia, which is famous for its ability to mimic human voices!

the bluebirds' nest. They sometimes destroy the eggs of a bluebird and even kill the nestlings.

House sparrows are not a protected bird in the United States. In their native home of England, however, these birds have recently been declining sharply in population, and some biologists are now worried that the house sparrow—the English sparrow—may become an uncommon sight in England.

If you can observe house sparrows in your neighborhood, watch for their behavior in small flocks. They flutter around

Let Me Introduce You . . .

By now, you might be confused about birds that are called nonnative. A native species is a bird that normally lives and nests in the wild in a certain area or country. Starlings, house sparrows (English sparrows), and pigeons were all species that were naturally wild in England or Europe. But once a species has become established in a new place, it is considered nonnative, because it has never been found in the wild there before.

Nonnative birds are often called **introduced** species. Many different species have been introduced to North America. The ring-necked pheasant, a native of Asia, is a good example. It was introduced into North America in the late 1800s. It was bred and raised as a game bird in several states and released in fields in the fall for hunters. It has also been introduced in Europe and Australia.

English sparrows and starlings are an introduced species in Australia. There are also tropical birds that have been raised in captivity as pets and accidentally escape—or are let loose when the owners don't want to care for them. In California, for example, there are small colonies of African bishop weaver finches. They have adapted well after escaping from the aviaries they were kept in (for breeding and to sell as pets). And in Florida, Texas, and California, several different species of colorful tropical parrots have now established nesting

groups. These birds were probably originally captive-raised and then escaped or were released—but survived in their new environment.

To add to the idea of birds living "in the wrong place," many birds are called accidentals when they are seen far from their normal breeding or wintering area. A bird might have been blown off course during its migration—by a huge hurricane or storm winds, for instance. On rare occasions, an American robin is seen in England. But accidentals do not stay to adapt and breed; they usually find their way back home.

Farms, Forests, and Fields

Visiting different habitats will give you a chance to see—and hear—many different species of birds. Eastern meadowlarks and bobolinks might be heard in the open fields or meadows around a farm. An American kestrel might be seen on a fence post at the edge of a field, hunting for mice. You are also likely to hear the crowing of a rooster at a farm or near the barn. Barn swallows and tree swallows can also be seen around farms, barnyards, and open fields.

At many farms, you will find chickens. That may not sound very exciting, but you can usually get fairly close to hens and

Chicken Chat

Today, just in the United States, there are many different breeds, or kinds, of chickens. Here are just a few:

- Andalusian
- Bantam
- Cornish
- Leghorn
- Orpington
- Plymouth Rock
- Polish crested
- Rhode Island Red
- Sussex
- Wyandotte

These different breeds and variations are not different species—they are all just domestic chickens, differing in color, size, patterns, comb shape, and egg size and color.

roosters and watch how they preen, eat, and drink. You will probably see them scratching out an area in the sand or dirt to take a dust bath. Listen to the different sounds that they make, especially when they are getting fed. Look at the top of the head of a rooster (the male) and then a hen (the female). The red, fleshy combs at the top are usually different: roosters have a larger, or taller comb and hens have a smaller, shorter comb. Most roosters have large,

spiky-looking "spurs" on their legs, and most hens do not. There's also usually an obvious difference in the shape of the tail between the two genders.

Chickens are domesticated birds. That means they are bred and raised in captivity, on farms and in poultry houses. All modern chickens are the descendants of a wild species, the red jungle fowl, native to India, China, and Indonesia. Jungle fowl were first domesticated more than 5,000 years ago!

They have been raised by people around the world and bred for size, color, patterns, and egg-laying.

Rhode Island Red chickens have been developed and raised in the eastern states for more than 100 years. In fact, it is such an important breed that it is the state bird of Rhode Island.

It sounds surprising that chickens were originally domesticated thousands of years ago, but other farm animals were also first tamed, bred, and kept by people thousands of years ago—goats, sheep, and horses are a few examples. All these domesticated animals have been an important part of human history.

Most states have weekend events such as "farm days" and "open farms" that allow the public to visit working farms. These events offer an opportunity to look at chickens, roosters, and domesticated ducks. Agricultural fairs and state fairs often have judged competitions for "best-in-show" chickens and ducks. You might also find an exhibit of newly hatched chicks!

On the Trail in Forest and Field

If you visit a nature center or wildlife sanctuary, there will probably be a choice

This Polish crested chicken is a breed sometimes seen at fairs. The topknot of feathers gives it an unusual appearance.

of hiking trails into the forest or wood-lands. Birds in dense woodlands are usu-ally hard to watch close-up, but you will still hear them singing and calling. The veery has a unique song that sounds like a downward spiral. The song is flutelike and goes down in tone, like a race down a spiral staircase. The black-throated green warbler also has a song that is easy to remember. It calls out *zee-zee-zoo-ZEET!* with great enthusiasm.

Many wildlife organizations, nature centers, and parks have "walk-and-talk" programs, which include bird-watching walks. A group leader who is an experi-enced birder will point out what to look for and will also identify the birdsongs and calls you hear.

Follow the Signs. Wildlife sanctuaries usually have a sign at the trailhead to let you know the rules about hiking, pets, or camping. Walking along any nature trail with a dog, even on a short leash, will likely frighten away birds and other wildlife. There may also be signs asking you not to feed the geese or ducks in the ponds.

Nature centers and sanctuaries often have wheelchair-accessible trails. You might also find trails that are wide and flat, which make it easier for anyone who has diffi-culty walking. And there may be a choice of short trails, if you don't have the ability to walk for very long. Look for signs that point out the different types of trails, or call ahead for information.

Have a Seat!

You will be able to get closer to birds if you don't move around much. In fact, many bird-watchers just sit down somewhere and wait for the birds to show up. Nature trails usually have benches to sit on, for people to just settle down to look at and listen to the wildlife. Even in a city park, it helps to sit quietly on a bench or a big rock. Sudden movement and sudden sounds are likely to scare away nearby birds. Good "bird man-ners" include not making loud noises and keeping your hands or arms still.

Detective Work

Even if you don't see or hear birds, you can look for signs of them. A short walk in a forest or a quick hike along a nature trail may disappoint you if no birds are around. But with a little detective work, you should be able to find some good clues.

Finding the Evidence. A lot of small body feathers on the ground, with larger wing or tail feathers nearby, probably means a bird has been killed. If you see this along a

---

Bird Worries

You might be surprised to find that some people don't want birds to be fed in public areas. They are concerned by the amount of droppings on the ground that a flock leaves, especially if there is also a pile of seed hulls. It all can leave quite a mess. And some people don't want to have big white splotches of bird drop-pings on their cars. In fact, some towns have laws about feeding large flocks in a public park or at a pond.

You may also discover that a friend or relative is truly terrified of birds (just like some people are very afraid of snakes or insects). That person might be afraid to go bird-watching with you. Let him or her know that you are only listening to birds and observing them and don't need to get close.

The small feathers covering a bird's body are called contour feathers. These are the feathers from a mourning dove (just slightly larger than a penny).

The feathers from this owl casting have been washed away by a heavy rainstorm, revealing the skull and other bones of a small bird that the owl ate.

Tracks, Feathers, and Castings

See if you can find the things birds leave behind.

Materials

✎ Just your eyes!

When birds are molting or preening, a loose feather will float to the ground. You might find a pigeon feather on a sidewalk or a crow or owl feather in the woods. Near houses, you may find a blue jay feather or a mourning dove feather.

Look for other evidence on the ground, such as castings of undigested food, white droppings, or an area with scratches in the sand where birds took a dust bath.

woodland trail, it could mean that a hawk has been hunting and struck its target. It may have carried its prey off to a large branch to pluck away some of the feathers before eating. If you see a burst of small feathers close to a house or other buildings, it probably means that a roaming housecat has killed a wild bird.

White bird droppings are easy to see. If you find white splotches on a city sidewalk, you can be sure there are some pigeons around. Round white splotches under a big oak or maple tree might be a clue to a roosting spot for a crow. Lots of chalky white splotches and splashes under a big pine or other evergreen tree might reveal that a hawk or owl nest is nearby. Take a look up in the tree to see if there is a large nest of twigs and sticks.

Hawk or owl castings are sometimes found on the ground, at the base of the tree that the bird was roosting in. Hawks and owls have to regurgitate (spit up) the fur, feathers, and bones of the prey they eat. They are spit out as a compact wad of material called a casting, or a pellet. If a hawk ate a brown sparrow, the casting would look like an oval or rounded mass of brown. If an owl ate gray mice, the casting would look like an oval gray pellet. If the castings have become wet in a heavy rain, you can see some of the bones in them—or even skulls!—because the rain has washed away the fur or feathers.

Please Note: Do not pick up or handle hawk or owl castings. They may have acquired bacteria or mold that could cause an illness or infection. It's best to take photos or make a drawing in your bird sketchbook and take written notes in your bird journal. Drawings and notes will give you a clue about where and when a hawk or owl may be using that tree for a roost. Always remember to write the date and place on your drawings.

Bird Tracks. Looking for evidence can include inspecting the snow during the winter or the sand on a beach. A thin layer of fresh snow is the best because the imprint of a bird's foot will be clear and sharp. Tracks of mourning doves and crows show up well, and you can easily see the marks of three forward toes and one hind toe. At the beach, the tracks of sandpipers and plovers near the water will show only three forward toes. The hind toe of many

shorebirds is so small that it doesn't leave a mark in the sand.

Dust Baths. Along a sandy dirt trail or at the edge of a lawn, you might see an area scraped away to make a circular or oval-shaped depression of loose, dry sand. Birds scratch at the loose dirt until they have made a dry "pool" of dusty dirt and sand. They settle down in the dust, fluff up their feathers, and then preen. If you find a dust bath and the weather remains dry, you will probably see birds return to it.

(left) The tracks of a mourning dove, in a light layer of snow.

(right) These are the tracks of shorebirds, probably small plovers, in the wet sand at a beach.

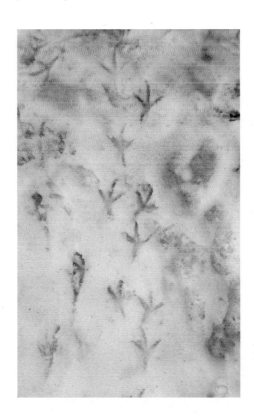

51

This ring-billed gull is one of many species of gulls that can be seen in coastal areas and on large lakes.

The male peafowl is called a peacock. It has beautiful iridescent feathers.

Oops! Not a Bird! Finding a lot of seed hulls on the ground (where people are feeding pigeons or other birds) is certainly a big clue that birds were eating there. But finding the hulls of sunflower seeds in a pile somewhere else might mean that a mouse, squirrel, or chipmunk (or even a human!) was eating the seeds. Chipmunks like to sit and eat on top of a rock or stump, where they leave seed hulls and half-eaten acorns. Red squirrels often take apart a pinecone piece by piece to get at the seeds and then leave the shreds in a pile.

Finding Last Season's Nests. If you live where most of the trees lose all their leaves in the fall, you're in luck! Take a close look up into the bare branches of trees and shrubs. You might see the remains of a nest from last summer, once the leaves are all gone. The birds that nested there will not use the same nest next year, but it will give you an idea of the types of trees and habitats in which birds nest. Nests that are close to the ground may be used during the winter by mice.

Go Visiting!

You can observe birds and listen to their songs in many public places. Here are a few examples:

- Public gardens: large flower gardens should give you a chance to watch hummingbirds as they hover from one bloom to another.

- Science museums or nature centers: these will probably have indoor exhibits about the local birds and may also have outdoor exhibits, trails, or guided tours.

- State and national parks: there will be hiking trails and probably a gift center with booklets or leaflets about the wildlife to be found there. There is usually a variety of habitat areas to visit, so you may see and hear several different species.

- Lake and seashore parks: ducks, geese, and swans are just a few types of water birds you might see. Gulls and terns may also be diving into the water for fish.

- City parks or animal parks: large public parks can give you the chance to observe some colorful nonnative birds, such as peacocks.

At the Zoo. If you have the opportunity to visit a large zoo or animal park, you can see birds from around the world. Large, flightless species such as the Australian

A Peacock's Scream!

Peacocks are called peafowl by ornithologists. They make a very loud noise!

Materials

- Just your ears!

Visit a place that has peacocks, such as a park or zoo. Peacocks are sometimes allowed to wander around a large park freely. They are native and wild in India but are often kept as beautiful (but noisy) specimens at parks and large private estates.

Males have long, beautiful tail feathers with colorful eyespots at the tip and iridescent, glossy feathers on their head and neck. Females (called peahens) are much duller in color and have shorter tails.

Watch to see how the peacocks react to each other as they wander around. Listen for their calls, which sound like a loud scream or screech.

Some parks and zoos may also have geese and turkeys; listen for them, too. You may be hearing quite a variety of sounds!

You might see an emu at the zoo. This is a young emu.

emu or the African ostrich might be kept in fenced areas.

A large aviary may house an African turaco (TOOR-ah-ko), a bird with a long rounded tail and a distinct crest. Smaller aviaries may have finches or parrots. There may be a water area or exhibit with penguins. Read all the signs so you know what species you are observing.

Your Own Backyard. The easiest place to find birds is in your own yard. Listen for bird sounds in the morning and again at the end of the day. If you live in the city, you'll probably hear pigeons (rock doves), English sparrows, and starlings. In suburban yards, you might hear mourning doves cooing, goldfinches twittering, and mockingbirds and blue jays squawking. If your home is near a woodland, you may hear chickadees, ovenbirds, nuthatches, and woodpeckers.

Go to School! Even at school, you might see a variety of birds. At the edge of the playground area or a playing field you might see chipping sparrows or robins feeding on the ground. There might be crows or swallows flying overhead. You might hear a catbird calling from a row of overgrown shrubs. A large puddle may attract some birds, especially in hot weather. And look at any fence to see if sparrows or other birds are perched along the top.

Finding Birds Indoors. You can find a surprising variety of species in your own home—in magazines, newspaper articles, on the television, and even on stamps! Look at the stamps on letters you get in the mail, and ask your friends and relatives to keep an eye out for any stamps with birds on them. If you have friends planning a vacation, ask them to look for interesting bird stamps while they travel.

(top) An emu is shown with a kangaroo on the Australian florin coin.

(left) This is an African Livingstone's turaco, a member of the cuckoo family.

Sketch Tropical Birds

Visiting a zoo or animal park gives you the perfect opportunity to add tropical birds to your bird sketchbook.

Materials

- Your bird sketchbook
- Colored pencils, crayons, or felt-tipped pens

1. Choose birds that have different shapes than what you are used to. A flamingo, for instance, has a very different shape from a robin. You might also see tropical birds you would never see at home, such as toucans, turacos, or large parrots.

2. Draw the birds as best you can. You might even draw in arrows to point out special field marks.

3. Write in the names of the birds, the date, and the place you visited. You may be able to stand and draw some large birds such as peacocks. They might be so used to seeing people all day that you can get quite close to them. There may be aviaries and flight cages that you can walk right up to and have a good view of the birds. Take your time, ask a zoo staff member questions, and take notes about the bird's feeding habits, behavior, and calls or songs.

You can easily add a variety of bird drawings to your sketchbook at a zoo or animal park. Although they aren't typically as colorful as tropical birds, pigeons and house sparrows wandering around make excellent "models" too, because you will probably be able to get close to them.

Stamps from around the world often have birds on them.

Draw a Territory Map

Add new information to your bird sketchbook by creating a territory map showing where a bird frequently feeds, sings, or nests.

Materials

- Your bird sketchbook
- Colored pencils, crayons, or felt-tipped pens

1. Select a defined area, or "territory," where you can bird-watch regularly, several times in one week. It could be your backyard, neighborhood park, school playground, or local zoo, among other places.

2. Look and listen for bird activity. Draw whatever you've discovered—a bird's-eye view of the area where you've found a nest, for example, or where you saw a pair of robins hunting for worms or grubs on a lawn.

3. Sketch in the main landmarks of the territory: a house, driveway, the largest tree, a garden or lawn, and a fence or hedge, for example.

4. Make an X in places where you have seen the birds feeding.

5. Make an S where you have heard the birds singing. A bird announcing its nesting territory will sing within the territory and also at the edges of it.

6. Make an arrow showing where you have spotted the nest or where you think there might be a nest.

7. Draw a dotted line that surrounds all the marked spots, and you will be able to get an idea of what most of that bird's territory looks like.

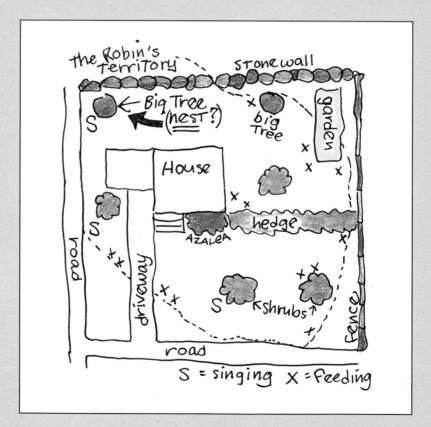

6

Dinnertime!

Birds come in all shapes and sizes—and so does their food. From tiny flies and caterpillars to snakes, fish, berries, seeds—and mice!—birds eat a wide variety of food.

Bugs for Breakfast

The American robin eats seeds, insects, berries, and earthworms. But the diet of many birds is almost entirely insects.

Swallows and martins catch insects on the wing—snapping them up in their beaks while they fly back and forth over fields and meadows. They eat horseflies, houseflies, flying ants, termites, flying beetles, may-flies, and grasshoppers. Barn swallows are found throughout North America, Great Britain, Europe, and Africa. They often follow people walking across fields and meadows or farmland, so they can eat the insects that are disturbed and fly up. Purple martins are such expert insect hunters that many people like to set up large nesting boxes for them—two-story houses with separate rooms for several different nesting pairs.

Chimney swifts, which build nests on the inside walls of old, unused chimneys, also feed mainly on insects; they snap them up as they fly, as swallows do. In Maine, a school in Brunswick and a nature sanctuary both have constructed nesting towers like tall, fake chimneys for the swifts to nest in. A nature center in Minnesota has built a tower for swifts, and there's one at a park in Winnepeg, Manitoba, in Canada. Swifts eat a lot of flying insects.

Woodland warblers also hunt for insects. The pine warbler feeds on moth larvae (caterpillars), grasshoppers, flies, beetles, and aphids. The common yellow-throat eats grasshoppers and beetles and also adds spiders to the list. Ovenbirds add centipedes, earthworms, and snails to their insect diet. The Canada warbler feeds on moths, beetles, grubs, mosquitoes, and caterpillars. Many warblers will also eat some berries, such as dogwood and sumac berries, and bayberry.

Phoebes, flycatchers, and kingbirds are insect hunters also. There are several species in Canada and the United States. They usually sit on a branch and then dart out to catch a passing insect. Pheobes eat

(left) Many birds eat insect larvae. This is a moth caterpillar.

(right) Wood-boring beetles like this are among the favorite insect foods of woodpeckers.

moths, especially those of the tent caterpillar, which can be very destructive to cherry trees.

Swallows, swifts, flycatchers, phoebes, and warblers all need to migrate south for the winter. Because they eat mostly insects, they would not be able to find food during the cold, snowy months when insects are inactive. They have to go where the food is!

Beetles and their larvae are the favorite food of most woodpeckers. All woodpeckers have beaks capable of chipping off the bark of dead trees and then pecking away at decaying wood to get at the insects inside.

Even though downy woodpeckers, hairy woodpeckers, and pileated woodpeckers feed on insects, they do not migrate south for the winter—because they can still find insect eggs and larvae. (The "mealworms" that pet shops sell for feeding birds are not true worms at all but the larvae of beetles.) Many people like to put out sunflower seeds and suet for the birds in the winter, and woodpeckers feed on those also.

Flickers are woodpeckers that like to feed on mostly ants. They can often be seen poking and pecking into stumps or on lawns, where there are ants. The acorn woodpecker of the western United States and Canada feeds on some insects—but it mostly collects and stores acorns to eat!

Seeds, Berries, and Fruit

Sparrows, finches, and thrushes eat a variety of seeds and berries, along with insects and spiders that they find while foraging on the ground. White-throated sparrows and fox sparrows both eat ragweed seeds—along with beetles and spiders. Song sparrows eat the seeds of knotweed, ragweed, and dandelion but also eat weevils, click beetles, grasshoppers, leaf hoppers, and termites. The beautiful northern cardinal is known to visit feeders during the winter for sunflower seeds or safflower seeds. But it also feeds on many different species of beetles, grasshoppers, and treehoppers, as well as spiders and slugs.

The seeds and fruit of shrubs are important autumn foods for some birds. Robins, catbirds, wild turkeys, and bluebirds eat the reddish berries of staghorn sumac. Dogwood berries are eaten by white-throated sparrows, wood ducks, ruffed grouse, cardinals, and evening grosbeaks. At coastal sites and lake areas, the waxy berries of bayberry shrubs are eaten by catbirds, pine warblers, and yellow-rumped warblers (also called myrtle warblers).

Other trees and shrubs are important also. The seeds of maple trees are eaten by evening grosbeaks and pine grosbeaks. The

The berries of dogwood are eaten by several species of birds. These are the berries of the gray-stemmed dogwood.

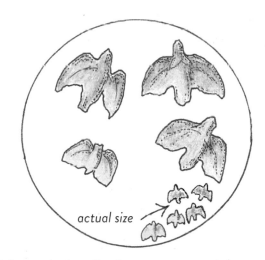
actual size

The seeds from birch trees are eaten by several species of birds.

Make a Juice Carton Feeder

A simple bird feeder made from a juice carton is sturdy enough to last through the winter.

Materials

Adult supervision required

- Scissors or knife
- Ruler
- Crayon or permanent marker
- Empty half-gallon juice carton, rinsed out
- 2 feet (61 cm) of strong string, twine, or cord or an old shoelace
- Sunflower seeds or other seed mix

1. Use a ruler and draw a 3-inch square on one side of the juice carton, with the bottom of the square about 2 inches from the bottom of the carton. Draw a matching square on the opposite side of the carton.

2. Draw a horizontal line across the middle of each square.

3. Cut along all lines except the top and bottom of each square. You may need to use a knife, so ask an adult to help you.

4. On both sides of the carton, fold down the bottom flap to make a landing place for birds. Fold up the top flap to make an awning or roof. The openings should line up so you can see through the carton.

5. Poke holes near the very top of the carton, as pictured. Ask an adult to help you to make the holes with the point of a knife or scissors.

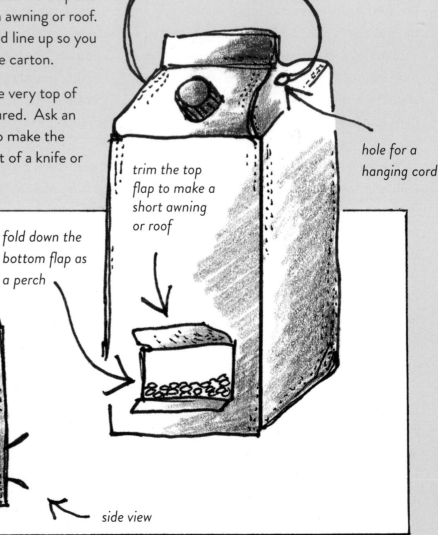

hole for a hanging cord

trim the top flap to make a short awning or roof

fold down the bottom flap as a perch

side view

6. Push a string or cord (or an old shoelace) through the holes.

7. Place sunflower seeds or a seed mix in the bottom of the carton.

8. Hang the feeder from a strong branch or hanger (as pictured).

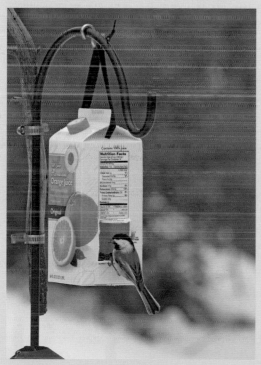

This black-capped chickadee is landing on a juice carton feeder to take a sunflower seed.

Make an Orange Feeder for Orioles

Orioles eat beetles, grasshoppers, spiders, and fruit, such as mulberries and wild black cherries. Orioles are also attracted to oranges, which you can cut in half and set out where they can peck at the juice and pulp.

Materials

Adult supervision required

- 1 ripe orange
- Knife
- Thin stick, such as a kabob skewer or plastic stirrer
- Strong cord

1. Cut an orange in half. You need only one half at a time.

2. Decide on a good site—somewhere you can place the orange securely, so it doesn't fall over.

3. Push a thin stick (or kabob skewer) through the center of the orange half. Ask an adult for help when using sharp objects.

4. Place the stick against a thick branch, fence, post, or railing to form a "t" or cross shape.

5. Use a strong cord to tie the stick to the branch or railing. Wrap the cord around the cross shape, back and forth, making an X shape. You may have to wrap the cord around several times. Another option is to use the cord alone to tie the orange half, cut side up, to a flat railing or sturdy branch. Make sure that the orange is securely fastened, so that if an oriole lands on it, it won't slip downward.

Orioles will come to feed at a ripe orange, cut in half.

(left) Seeds will develop in the center disks of these sunflowers as fall approaches. The seeds will attract chickadees, finches, and nuthatches.

(right) The flowers of red monarda are one of the favorite food plants of hummingbirds. Monardas are also called bee balm or Oswego tea.

Flower Power

Hummingbirds hover in front of flowers while they sip nectar. They can also fly backward and away from the plant they are feeding at!

Many different garden plants, especially those with long, tubelike red flowers, attract hummingbirds, including:

- Cardinal flower
- Red monarda
- Blue lobelia
- Red trumpet-creeper
- Red columbine
- Scarlet runner bean
- Red salvia
- Cleome
- Sage

berries of hawthorns are favored by fox sparrows and cedar waxwings. There are at least 100 species of hawthorns in North America, and many **cultivated** varieties are used for landscaping. The berries of viburnum are also eaten by many different species.

The seeds from birch trees are eaten by redpolls, pine siskins, goldfinches, and grouse. The seeds are produced in dangling catkins—narrow clusters up to two inches long—that break apart and fall to the ground. Each separate seed has a shape like a tiny winged bird!

Seeds from garden plants are important also. Goldfinches will jump onto the tall stalks of leonurus plants that have gone to seed—they make the stalks bend to the ground so they can get at the seeds. In the fall, one of the biggest attractions in any garden is a tall sunflower. The center of the flower head is a dark disk bearing lots of seeds. If you plant a few sunflowers in the spring, you are likely to see goldfinches, chickadees, and nuthatches clinging to the dried flower heads in the fall, picking out the seeds in the center. (Follow the instructions for planting on a pack of sunflower seeds. Don't try to plant the seeds from a bag of birdseed. You'll end up with a different type of flower.)

Snakes for a Snack and Lizards for Lunch

It might be hard to imagine a bird hunting for snakes, but the broad-winged hawk is notable for its ability to catch and eat small snakes. This hawk is not as large as some others—its wingspan is barely 35 inches across (88.9 cm). It hunts mice and also moths, beetles, grasshoppers, spiders, frogs, lizards, snakes—and crayfish!

In the southwestern United States, the roadrunner (a type of cuckoo made famous in cartoons) often catches small snakes and lizards. The roadrunner and broad-winged hawk are not the only birds that eat lizards. The Harris's hawk of the American Southwest hunts for mice, rats, and gophers,

A female ruby-throated hummingbird rests on a twig. Only the males have red throat feathers.

Plant Flowers That Attract Hummingbirds

You can plant red monarda flowers to attract hummingbirds. The flowers will do well in a large pot or can be planted in the ground.

Materials

- Gardening gloves or work gloves
- Trowel
- Pot of red monarda or other plants from the list on p. 62 (You can often find seedlings in small pots from a garden store.)

1. Put on gardening gloves to protect your hands. Using the trowel, dig a hole deep enough for the size of the pot.

2. Hold the pot sideways. Squeeze it a little to help remove the dirt, the plant, and its roots all together in one clump.

3. Put the pot aside and set the plant and dirt into the hole, and fill in around it with dirt you removed earlier. Lightly press the dirt down around it.

4. Water the plant.

It may take a few weeks for the monarada to grow flower buds, so it's best to plant them in the spring—but after any danger of a frost. You can also try planting flowers from seed. You will need to read the instructions on the back of the seed package.

An American kestrel perches at the edge of a field, waiting to spot a grasshopper or a mouse.

The northern saw-whet owl, only about eight inches (20.3 cm) long, hunts for mice in the forest at night.

but its prey also includes lizards. Lizards are hunted by the Swainson's hawk too, although it usually hunts mice, gophers, voles, and even grasshoppers.

Hover and Dive

Although hummingbirds are amazing in their ability to hover, hovering in place is a necessary maneuver for other birds also. An osprey can briefly hover over the water before it spots a fish and dives. Terns and gulls do the same thing.

The American kestrel is a small falcon—about the size of a robin—that eats a variety of prey. It often sits on a fence post or large branch at the edge of a field or meadow, waiting to see a mouse below. Then it flies out, hovers briefly over the spot where the mouse is, and then dives down to catch it. Kestrels also eat moles and small rats but feed on insects too, including a lot

Mice (*left*) and voles (*right*) look similar, but voles have tiny ears and much shorter tails.

of grasshoppers, beetles, and crickets. The European kestrel, similar to the American kestrel, is a different species but is also known for its hovering ability. It is sometimes called the windhover in England.

Lots of Mice. Kestrels eat many mice, but owls hunt for rodents also. Most owls are nocturnal (active during the night), but the barred owl, found in southern Canada and the eastern half of the United States, is sometimes active on cloudy, dim days. It hunts mostly mice but also feeds on rats, squirrels, small birds, frogs, insects, and spiders. The hooting call of the barred owl is easy to remember: it sounds like "Who cooks for youuu? Who cooks for youu alll?"

The screech owl, a small owl barely nine inches (22.9 cm) long, catches mostly mice at night but also eats spiders, insects, and even earthworms. Another small owl, the saw-whet, hunts mostly mice, rats, shrews, and even bats!

The red-tailed hawk, common throughout much of Canada and the United States, hunts for mice and voles (often called meadow mice) in fields. The marsh hawk, skimming over marshy fields and wet, grassy meadows, also eats mice and voles. Voles look like mice but have tiny ears and a very short tail. Voles are also very different from moles.

Fast Food

Several species of hawks and falcons hunt for and eat smaller birds. The peregrine falcon is known by a common name—the duck hawk—because ducks are sometimes its prey. Peregrines also hunt pigeons, starlings, sparrows, mourning doves, plovers, quail, and many other species of birds. A peregrine needs to be very fast to be able to hunt and kill its prey. It has been estimated that the downward "stoop" of a peregrine falcon as it plummets toward its prey is about 160 to 180 miles per hour! The falcon isn't flying that fast—it's diving, with its wings nearly closed.

The group of forest hawks known as "short wings" includes the sharp-shinned hawk, goshawk, and Cooper's hawk. They all have somewhat short, rounded wings that allow them to make fast, dashing flights through the forest to catch their prey. The smallest of the three is the sharp-shin, which is only about 11 inches (28 cm) long—the size of a blue jay. It feeds on doves, sparrows, thrushes, and other smaller birds but also eats a variety of beetles, moths, grasshoppers, and even caterpillars. The Cooper's hawk is larger than the "sharpie" and hunts for doves, grackles, thrushes, and other birds but also eats rats,

This black-bellied plover has found a large marine worm at the water's edge. It was photographed during the winter, before molting into new plumage. In the summer, it will have new black feathers on its belly.

mice, and squirrels. The goshawk is the largest short wing, about 20 inches (50.8 cm) in length. An adult "gos" is silver-gray with ruby-red eyes. Its avian prey includes ducks, pigeons, grouse, quail, and blue jays, but it also catches mice and squirrels. All three short-winged hawks are masters at speeding through a forest, zooming around trees and branches to catch their prey.

Going Fishing

Many birds feed on fish. The osprey catches fish in shallow water, diving in to grab its prey with its sharp, curved talons. It hunts in lakes, in the ocean along the shore, and at estuaries (where rivers run out to the sea). Bald eagles also feed mostly on fish but are able to catch other prey such as muskrats, squirrels, and rats.

Gulls and terns eat fish also, hovering and diving along the coastline or in bays and lakes. Herons, egrets, and bitterns all have long beaks that they use to catch fish—along with the occasional frog or large insect. And loons, puffins, cormorants, and gannets also feed chiefly on fish.

It's Not Moving . . .

Vultures eat carrion (dead animals). They are **scavengers**, looking for any animals that have been killed by cars along the roads, have drowned in storms, or are otherwise dead. Vultures circle and soar high above, with wings spread out in a wide, flat V-shape. When they find food, several vultures may float down to eat together. The movement of their black feathers as they feed sounds like the rustle of silk. Their dinner of carrion might include mammals such as squirrels or raccoons or smaller animals such as frogs or turtles squashed on the road—and even dead tadpoles, if a small pond has dried up and left the tadpoles stranded. As long as it's not moving, it will probably be cleaned up by these useful big birds. Vultures are a sort of "cleaning crew," keeping the landscape free of decaying carrion.

At the Beach

Shorebirds such as sandpipers and plovers are often seen in small flocks along beaches that are protected as sanctuaries. They hunt for food along the water's edge and in the seawrack—the line of washed-up seaweed, starfish, mussel shells, and crabs. In the mix of seawrack, the birds find insects and marine worms to eat. There are also plenty of crustaceans: small isopods (which look like woodland sowbugs) and amphipods, often called sandhoppers (which look like tiny shrimp). Flies and beetles are often in the seawrack also and are eaten. Sandpipers and plovers quickly run back and forth along the water's edge and the line of seawrack to pick out all these tiny creatures with their beaks. They need to feed on safe beaches, where there is no interference from people or their pets. It is a wonderful experience to have the chance to watch these birds from a distance as they feed.

 LOOK FOR

How Birds Drink and Bathe

If you have set out a water pan or have a birdbath that you can watch from a window, it's easy to observe bird behavior. Sometimes, two or three birds "line up" to wait for a bath! You could also watch from an outdoor seat, just far enough away so that birds are not frightened but close enough that it's still easy to watch them.

Materials

↘ Just your eyes!

Observe the different ways a bird drinks. Most birds dip their beaks in the water and then lift their heads up. But pigeons and doves put their beaks in and seem to suck the water up instead. On a hot summer day, birds may take several drinks at one time. A bird might jab or bite at the water first before drinking, as if to test it. Most birds that decide to bathe will test the water by drinking first, then stepping carefully into the pan. They will vigorously fluff their feathers, wiggle their wings, and shake their body all over, even putting their head in the water—it's quite a performance! Then they will hop out and look for a place to preen and dry safely.

Grit and Gravel

Most small birds need to have sand, tiny pebbles, and other grit in their diet, to help grind up the seeds and hard parts of plants that they eat. Even pet birds such parakeets need to have grit and a calcium block or cuttlefish bone in their cage to peck at. If you have never kept a pet bird, take a look at the bird supplies in a pet store, and you'll see the choices available for cage birds. You'll also find boxes of "bird gravel" that contain ground oyster shells for calcium that pet birds need. People who like to feed wild birds often put out sand and calcium grit for birds, especially in the winter or early spring. You can sprinkle grit on the ground in a few different areas where you have seen birds feed and see what species come to it. Because grit is usually light in color, the birds can spot it easily.

Safely Snacking and Wonderful Water

Wherever birds feed or look for food, they need safe "cover"—trees, shrubs, or brush piles where they can rest or preen in safety. After feeding, drinking, bathing, or getting grit, birds usually hop or fly to nearby cover.

Set Up a Birdbath or Water Pan

You can attract birds by setting out a shallow pan or tray of water.

Materials

- Shallow pan such as an old cake pan, not more than 2 inches (5 cm) deep. Or, use a flower-pot tray: the flat, shallow tray or pan that's used under a flower pot so it won't drip when watered. This should also be less than 2 inches (5 cm) deep.
- A few large pebbles or a flat rock

1. Choose a good site to place the bath. The ground should be level. There should be some evergreens or other shrubs nearby. Pick a site where you can easily watch the birds from a window.

2. Set the pan or tray down and fill it with water. Be sure the water is only about an inch (2.5 cm) to an inch and a half (3.8 cm) deep.

3. Toss in a few large pebbles or a flat stone. These will give the birds confidence to enter the water because it will help them judge how deep the water is.

During the winter in cold areas, you will want to supply fresh water whenever the pan is frozen over. Although birds do eat snow in the winter when natural ponds and pools are frozen solid, they still enjoy coming to a water pan for a drink!

Evergreen shrubs and trees are often choice safety zones. An evergreen hedge is usually a safe place. Loose brush piles also provide excellent protection. These places even allow a bird to take a short nap in safety!

If a bird's feathers are wet, it cannot fly well. So after a bath, birds usually fly to a safe place where they can spend some time preening their feathers. One way of attracting birds is to set out a birdbath or shallow pan of water. Even a flat rock that has a depression in the center where you can pour water will attract birds that want to get a drink or take a bath.

Birds are constantly in danger from predators and difficult weather conditions. Natural predators, such as hawks, might suddenly zoom by, looking for prey. But there are often additional dangers, such as roaming cats or dogs. Birds also need to find shelter against bad weather such as sleet, heavy winds, or pouring rain. Chickadees, bluebirds, and woodpeckers may use an old nesting site in a tree hole or birdhouse, but other birds often find cover in a stand of evergreens.

Safe feeding, roosting, bathing, and preening sites are very important to the survival of any bird. Trees and shrubs, especially evergreens, provide safety zones for all these activities.

7

Travel Time!
(Got Geography?)

If you live in Canada or the northern part of the United States, you probably have already noticed that most of your "summer birds" leave your area at the end of the nesting season. They migrate south, flying to warmer climates where there is more food. They can't survive the winter months in their summer breeding area because most of the insects or plant food are gone. And they would not be able to survive the freezing and below-freezing temperatures!

The Shorebird Migration

At the end of the nesting season—usually around early August—shorebirds in northern areas gather to head south. They may flock together in large numbers, especially along beaches that are protected sanctuaries. They need to eat a lot of food before they leave. Small sandpipers can be seen running around at the water's edge or near the seawrack along the tide line. Plovers group together in flocks to feed furiously before they take flight. Long-legged species such as

(left) Sanderlings run along the beach, finding food in the seawrack or along the water's edge.

(right) This ruddy turnstone is molting and losing its summer feathers.

willets and yellowlegs can be seen in marshy areas and estuaries. They need to find shorelines and beaches that are safe for feeding.

Sanderlings, purple sandpipers, and ruddy turnstones nest in far northern Canada—close to the Arctic Circle or even above it! So flying south for them means heading for the coastline of the United States.

Turnstones spend winters on the shores of the Atlantic, from Maine to Florida, and farther down to Mexico. Purple sandpipers, which also nest in northern Canada, migrate to the eastern coast of Newfoundland and also down to Florida. Shorebirds often gather in large numbers as they get ready to migrate. For example, on just one day, bird-watchers on the coast of Massachusetts counted:

- 600 black-bellied plovers together at one beach area
- 800 sanderlings gathered near a bay
- 1,000 semipalmated plovers on Plum Island

Ducks and geese also gather together in enormous flocks before they take off on their migration flights. Hundreds may be seen in flocks at lakes, estuary marshes, and bays. Bird-watchers often travel, too—to coastal sanctuaries where they can observe big flocks of migrants. Some parks and sanctuaries even have raised platforms, special roadways, and observation sites for bird-watchers to look out onto the water's edge.

A flock of shorebirds in flight.

A small flock of Canada geese.

Look at a world map and find the Arctic Circle. (Ask your teacher, librarian, or parent to help you.) You'll have a better idea of just how big a trip it is to fly from the Arctic to the southern United States!

Honk and Quack

Canada geese are familiar birds along lakes, coastal areas, open marshes, and fields—and even parks and golf courses. They nest across most of Canada and much of the United States and migrate south in the autumn. A slightly smaller goose called the brant nests in Greenland and the Canadian Arctic, and heads down to

Geese and Ducks Honking and Quacking

Ducks and geese call to each other as they fly. Learn to "spot" them with your ears.

Materials

 Just your ears!

Whenever you are at a park, zoo, or sanctuary, listen for the sounds of geese and ducks. Learning to recognize their calls will help to alert you if you hear these birds as they fly overhead during migration. Sometimes you can hear the flock advancing as they call to each other from high above.

71

(left) A brant goose. Brant nest in the Arctic and migrate south to spend the winter along both the Atlantic and Pacific coasts in the United States.

(right) A wood duck. This is a male. Females are mostly brown. Note that it has a band on its leg, which is used by bird banders to identify the bird and gather data.

the shores of New Jersey and the Carolinas in the United States for the winter—a distance of at least 3,000 miles. Brant also travel to the Pacific coast. Geese are easy to notice as they gather in flocks in lakes or along shores. They are also easy to hear when they fly overhead in formation! Geese make "honk honk" calls to each other as they fly. Migrating flocks often fly in a long V formation or long uneven lines, honking as they fly. There may be as many as 73 geese in just one V formation!

Many species of ducks migrate south. The American wigeon spends the summer

months in the north-central United States and central Canada and then flies south to Texas, the southeast coast to Florida, and to Mexico and even Cuba. One of the most beautiful ducks in the world is the wood duck, which nests in parts of southeast and central Canada and the northeastern United States. It migrates to the southeast United States and into Mexico for the winter.

Like geese, ducks often call as they fly, quacking frequently to each other as they wing their way south.

An American wigeon. This is a male. The head of a female is mostly gray-brown.

Hawk Watch!

Most hawks and falcons fly to southern areas for the winter months. A broad-winged hawk from Nova Scotia or Maine may fly south to Central America. A Cooper's hawk from central Canada might migrate down to the southern United States. When the wind and weather are just right, there are large southward flights of hawks—and they can be seen from a mountain, ridge, or open field, flying by, one after another. Bird-watchers also flock there and count birds as they go by. At a

"hawk watch" on Cape Cod, 11 red-tailed hawks, 14 kestrels, and a peregrine falcon were seen on just one count day.

Some places are well known for the huge numbers of hawks and falcons that pass by each autumn. One famous site is Hawk Mountain Sanctuary in Pennsylvania. Hawk-watchers can sit on the top of a ridge and count the birds as they speed by or soar overhead. More than 15,000 hawks and falcons are counted each fall!

The broad-winged hawk is an exceptional traveler. These birds often gather together in large, swirling groups called a

V-Shaped Flocks

Now that you've learned to recognize the honking and quacking of ducks and geese, you can quickly look up to find the V formation or long line of birds as they go by.

Materials

 ✄ Just your eyes!

After gathering together in flocks, ducks and geese fly in a V-shaped formation to migrate south. When you hear them, look up and notice these variations: you may see long, straggling lines instead of a V shape. Ducks often fly in small groups of just four or five. The flocks may be so high up they just look like a pattern of floating dots in the sky, going overhead.

If your sense of direction is good, or if you have a compass, try to figure out if the flock is headed straight north—or south.

(left) A peregrine falcon is an exciting and memorable sight when observed on migration.

(right) A black-throated green warbler may migrate as far south as Guatemala and Costa Rica in Central America. This is a male.

kettle. The kettle of hawks takes advantage of a rising column of air, called a **thermal**, to gain altitude. The upward gust of the thermal helps them to gain height, so they can glide away with less effort than flapping. Turkey vultures are also seen in kettles, swirling and circling as they gain altitude.

Sanctuaries and birding groups often have hawk watch days—usually in October—so that bird-watchers can gather to count the hawks and falcons when the wind and weather are just right. People gather along a ridge, hilltop, or mountain to count the hawks and report the day's totals. When a rare or unusual sighting occurs—such as a peregrine falcon—everyone is happy and excited, and the falcon's flight is the highlight of the day. An osprey or eagle migrating by also makes for a memorable hawk watch day.

Warbler Week

Most larger migrants, such as ducks, geese, and hawks, are easy to observe during the fall migration as they head south. But in the spring, when birds return to the North, it is small birds such as warblers that become the celebrities. In fact, some bird clubs, parks, and sanctuaries even host special "warbler watch" days. In the northern states, bird-watchers look forward to "warbler week," usually the first and second week of May. The leaves on most trees are not yet fully opened, so it is easier to see the warblers as they forage for insects on the branches.

So many warblers and other small birds migrate in May that International Migratory Bird Day celebrations are held on the second Saturday of May each year in North America. Many nature centers and parks participate, hosting warbler walks and other events.

Dangers on the Wing

Birds face many hazards when they are migrating. Some of the most deadly are communication towers for cell phones and tall buildings with a lot of windows. Birds accidentally fly into these at night or when disoriented by storms. Millions of birds are killed this way each year in North America. Other hazards include storms, relentless rain, and oil spills on coastlines.

Birds are also killed in the daytime, when they fly into windows of smaller buildings, such as schools, homes, or offices. The glass reflects the branches of nearby trees or the sky, making the birds think that they can fly through it.

Many bird-watchers and naturalists like to place window-guards on their windows so birds don't try to fly through them. One easy method is to press a sheet of plastic wrap across the center of the window on the outside, leaving some wrinkles in it. That reduces the reflection. Another method is to use a bar of soap to draw designs all over a window (which can be washed away so you can make new designs whenever you want). These methods will usually work, as long as they keep the window from looking perfectly clear. Any

Make a Window Guard

Window guards can prevent migrating birds from seeing the reflection of branches or the sky on your windowpane and thinking they can fly through it.

Materials

- Pencil
- White or colored paper (but not blue, which a bird might mistake for the sky, and not green, like leaves)
- Scissors
- Tape

1. Think about some designs and sketch them on the paper. Here are a few ideas:

   ➤ Snowflake designs—white, or even in color, like purple!

   ➤ Swirling, curly, wavy patterns.

   ➤ Geometric shapes, diamonds, or zigzags.

2. Cut out your designs.

3. Tape them to the window—either inside or outside is okay, but hanging them inside will protect them from rain, wind, and snow.

4. Go outside and look at the window. Does your design break up most of the reflection from the sky?

pattern or cutout design that breaks up the reflection is a good solution.

Don't Wander Off Too Far!

Although most insect-eating birds in the North have to travel as far as South America to spend the winter, many species of birds don't migrate at all. These species are often called year-round **residents**. Chickadees, cardinals, and woodpeckers usually stay in the general area of their summer nesting territory. Crows, blue jays, and English sparrows also tend to remain in the same area. All these birds may expand their range a little in the winter as they search for food or look for good roosting places, but they don't usually travel too far away.

(left) A snowy owl, the official provincial bird of Quebec, Canada.

(right) A barn swallow in flight.

Some birds travel only as far as they need to, to find a good food supply. In parts of the United States, American robins are frequently seen all winter long, as long as there are sumac berries or other food nearby.

During severe and difficult winters, owls from Canada sometimes make a short migration down to the northern United States to find food. For example, heavy snowfalls can force snowy owls from Canada to fly to southern Maine or to

Minnesota for better hunting. A "snowy" may be seen sitting on rocks at the edge of a marsh or open field, waiting for mice or voles. They are even seen at airports, near the open areas of airfields. At one airport in Massachusetts, so many snowy owls show up in the winter that they are sometimes trapped and released somewhere else! The sighting of snowies often creates a stir among bird-watchers. The owl may stay in the area for several days, giving people

a chance to see a species that they would normally have to travel to the Arctic to see. The native Inuit peoples of Alaska call the snowy owl "okpik."

How Far? How Fast?

The barn swallows you observe during the summer months fly south to spend the winter in South America. Some go to Argentina, some fly to Bolivia. They have to travel as far as 6,000 miles to get to their wintering grounds. Then they have to fly back in the spring!

A pine warbler nesting in southeastern Canada may migrate south to Louisiana or Texas in the fall. A palm warbler that nested in central Canada during the summer would migrate down to Panama or even Cuba—a distance of about 3,000 miles. Other warblers migrate even farther: the black-throated green warbler flies as far south as Guatemala, the Caribbean, and Costa Rica.

Broad-winged hawks from Canada and the United States fly south in the fall and might spend the winter as far away as Mexico, Panama, or Venezuela. However, many individuals do not fly that far if they find enough food in the southern United States.

A broad-winged hawk passes overhead on migration. This is a juvenile, hatched earlier in the spring. On its next migration, its tail will have broad black and white bands across it.

Amazing Migrants. Several species, like the swallows, are notable for their long-distance travels. Godwits, which are large, long-billed shorebirds, migrate more than 6,000 miles to get to their wintering areas. The arctic tern, which nests as far north as Greenland and the Canadian Arctic, flies south over the Atlantic Ocean, past the tip of South America—sometimes even to the edge of Antarctica—and then comes back up north in the spring for nesting again in the Arctic. The round-trip is more than 20,000 miles!

Shearwaters also travel enormous distances and probably fly even more miles than the arctic terns.

Speedy Flights

It's not easy to judge how fast a bird flies while on migration, but there are some good estimates:

- Ducks usually fly along at 40 to 50 miles per hour.

- Most other birds go at a lesser speed—about 25 to 30 miles per hour.

- Small birds, such as flycatchers, fly at only about 10 to 20 miles per hour.

These estimates are made several ways, including using the same kind of radar equipment that local police use to find out if a car is speeding. You can estimate a bird's flight speed yourself. The next time you are in a car, ask the driver how fast the car is going. Then if you see that a flying bird is keeping up with the speed of the car—or passing it—you have a good idea how fast that bird is flying.

An amazing feat of flying is performed by the ruby-throated hummingbird. It heads south for the winter, flying to Florida and the Gulf Coast, and then flies across the Gulf of Mexico—across the open water of the Gulf—a distance of nearly 600 miles. But that's not all. The tiny hummingbird must survive to fly back that distance all over again, to return to its nesting territory in the spring. And if it lives to be three or four years old, it will be making those amazing flights each year!

Flocking, Feeding, Resting, and Roosting

When shorebirds, ducks, and geese land anywhere along their migration southward, they need to feed and rest safely. In both Canada and the United States, there are many coastal sanctuaries, bays, and estuaries that are protected places. These beaches usually have restricted areas where human activity is not allowed. Shorebirds that land exhausted and hungry on public beaches

White-throated sparrows often hop into brush piles to rest and preen.

are sometimes frightened away by people jogging or playing on the beach or loose dogs romping around. The birds cannot land, and they have to try again to look for a safe place. That's why there are sanctuaries, parks, and protected beaches for migrating shorebirds and ducks.

Small birds need safe roosting and feeding places also. They may look for a grove of pine trees or other evergreens or thickets of bushes and shrubs. Brush piles also make a good resting place. During the spring and fall migrations, several species of small birds like to hide or rest in brush piles of big branches and twigs: song sparrows, white-throated sparrows, chipping sparrows, and juncos, to name just a few.

Build a Brush Pile for Small Birds

A loose pile of branches and sticks makes a perfect roosting place for birds on the go. It's a safe stopover after birds have made a long flight or need to rest or preen.

Materials

- Work gloves or gardening gloves
- Your bird journal
- A pen or pencil

1. Choose a site at the edge of a lawn, woods, or weedy area.

2. Gather up tree branches that fork into smaller twigs. Try to find large ones that are at least four or five feet (1.2 to 1.5 m) long.

3. Pile the branches together in a loose collection so that some of them stick up higher at the top. It will look more inviting for a bird to perch on and look all around to see if it is safe.

4. Keep an eye on the brush pile and watch to see which birds show up. Notice whether they sit at the very top (song sparrows are likely to do that) or whether they hop into or under the branches. You can watch from a window, from the inside of a car, or you can even just sit quietly 10 or 20 feet away (pigeons and English sparrows usually don't mind if you're that close). Add your observations to your bird journal.

8

Bird Workers

Many people work in different ways to protect birds and their natural habitats. Bird banders provide information on where and when birds migrate—so we know which species need special protection or what areas should become sanctuaries. Wildlife rehabilitators rescue and care for injured birds. Conservationists evaluate land and seashore habitats that need to be preserved. And volunteers participate in Christmas bird counts or winter census counts at feeders, helping to establish data on wintering bird populations.

Bird Banders at Work

All across the United States and Canada, biologists and research volunteers work at bird-banding stations. A bird is trapped, usually in a net, and a metal band is put on its leg. Each band has tiny numbers printed on it. The bird bander writes down information about the bird, and then it is released.

To become a bird bander, a person must get special training to learn how to trap, band, and collect the data needed. He or she must have recommendations from other professional wildlife workers. After the person is trained, he or she must apply for federal and state permits. Bird banders usually work at a nature center or research group that has a banding station.

Here are some other details about bird banding:

⅄ Licensed bird banders often have volunteers who help them.

⅄ The nets used are called mist nets, so named because they are made of such fine netting that you—and the birds—can hardly see them! The mist nets are long, like a tennis or badminton net, and are very light and delicate, so they don't hurt the birds. Birds flying past become tangled in the fine netting. They are very carefully removed and brought to the banding station.

⅄ A metal or metal-alloy band is put on the bird's leg. The band is loose and can move freely—like a person wearing a bracelet. It does not hurt the bird or get in the way of feeding, preening, or nesting. Each band has a different number.

⅄ Each bird is weighed, inspected for feather condition, and will even have ticks or other parasites removed.

⅄ Wings are measured. Eye color is noted.

⅄ The bander determines if the bird is male or female and if it is a young bird—hatched in the past year—or older.

⅄ As soon as all the data is recorded, the bird is released.

All this information is sent in to the federal program in Maryland.

(left) This bird has just been banded at a wildlife sanctuary.

(right) A bird bander expertly removes a catbird from a mist net.

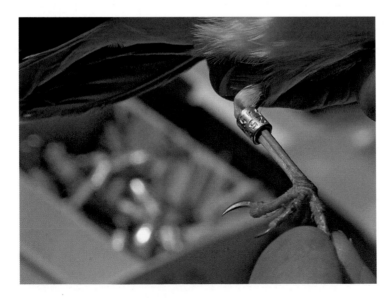

And Then What Happens? After a bird is banded and released, it may be trapped again the next day or week—or even many years later—by another bird bander in a different area. Because each band has a different number, researchers can tell where and when the bird was originally banded. Over the course of even a few years, there may be a lot of data written by the bird banders who recover the same individual bird.

Data gathered about birds that are retrapped give scientists a lot of information. Researchers can find out how long birds live and if a species is becoming more common or if the population is decreasing. The data might reveal an area that is important for large flocks of migrating birds. A woodland or seashore may need to have a sanctuary established. Scientists can even find out if males and females migrate to different places or at different times.

Not Just Banding. Some large birds are not banded but have numbered tags put on their wings instead. California condors (which have a wingspan of about 10 feet [3 m] across) have wing tags with large numbers printed on them. Biologists can read the number on a condor's tag with binoculars and know "who" that individual is and if the bird is safe, alive, and well. Condors

These eastern phoebe nestlings were brought to a wildlife rehabilitation center when their nest fell down.

are extremely rare, so it is important to know how each one is doing.

In Australia, young pelicans are captured and given wing tags so researchers can find out where and when they spend the seasons.

Wildlife Rehabilitators

Birds that have been injured or nestlings that have had their nest destroyed are cared for by wildlife rehabilitators. Rehabilitators have federal permits to rescue and take care of wild animals or raise young animals. Some rehabilitators specialize in taking care of birds. Most "rehab" workers have

jobs at nature centers, science centers, zoos, or parks. They usually rely on volunteers to help them take care of the birds. A single wildlife center may care for hundreds—or even close to 1,000—birds in just one year! Across the United States and Canada, there are people who have permits to take care of wild birds because so many are injured or left without a nest. Here are a few of the most common reasons that birds are taken to a wildlife rehabilitation center:

- A bird has been hit by a car when it flies low across the road. This happens especially with owls when they try to catch a mouse running across a road at night.

- A bird has been clawed and bitten by a housecat and then left injured or dying.

- A nest on the ground has been destroyed by a dog or cat—or even a lawn mower cutting through tall field grasses.

- A tree has been cut down in late spring while there was a nest in it.

- A hunter has shot a hawk (which is against the law) and its wing is broken.

- A bird has flown into a window and has damaged a wing or leg.

Every summer, these events bring injured birds to wildlife rehab stations. Most are given care and food and then are released when they are well. Many do not survive being injured by cats. Researchers estimate that hundreds of millions of birds are killed each year in the United States by loose housecats.

Birds that are shot or hit by cars often die. Hawks and owls that have a permanently damaged wing will never fly or hunt again. They are kept in large outdoor flight cages and are cared for by the bird workers at the rehab center. A hawk or owl that has been tamed may be taken to schools as an educational "ambassador," to explain how birds are injured and how they are cared for.

Most wildlife rehab stations also need volunteers to help take care of the birds. There is no day off from the constant care, because baby birds need to be fed every day, from dawn to dusk. Even a hawk or owl in a large flight cage needs to be fed every day. Bird workers always have something to do: prepare food, clean the

(below) This purple gallinule is being cared for at a wildlife rehab center. Its normal range is in the American Southeast—but it was found in Maine! It was blown far off course by a severe storm.

(right) This barred owl has a damaged wing that will never heal properly. It cannot survive in the wild. But rehabilitators have tamed it so it can be brought to classrooms.

nest boxes that baby birds are kept in, clean larger cages or aviaries, and take emergency phone calls.

Other accidents also occur, bringing in more birds that need care:

- A severe storm or hurricane may injure birds.

- Storm winds may blow a migrant off course, far away from its normal path.

- In early spring, insect-eating birds are just arriving back north in their nesting areas. A sudden, late snowstorm with freezing temperatures, however, can keep birds from finding food.

- An oil spill along the coast can coat waterbirds with oil. They cannot preen the oil from their feathers or fly or dive in the water for food. Rehab workers have to clean off each individual bird.

- Pesticides or other chemicals were sprayed on insects or plants, killing birds or making them too sick to fly or eat.

Laws to Protect Birds

Wild migratory birds are protected by federal and international laws. It is against the law to collect the nests, eggs, or even

Falconry Facts

There are special federal and state permits for falconers, who train hawks and falcons to hunt game. Falconry is such a difficult and demanding way of hunting that few people become falconers. There are very strict regulations on how the hawks are housed, fed, and exercised. A few airports even use trained falcons to frighten other birds away from runways to make it safe for airplanes to take off and land.

These rocky cliffs are found at Gros Morne National Park in Newfoundland, Canada. Large parks and sanctuaries protect habitat areas.

Sanctuary Habitats

You might be surprised at the variety of habitats found at some nature parks.

Materials

↘ Just your eyes!

If you visit a sanctuary or nature park, look for trail signs or use a trail map to find different habitats. There may be areas marked as:

- ➤ Salt marsh or wetlands
- ➤ Forests
- ➤ Open fields or meadows
- ➤ Streams, rivers, or ponds
- ➤ Rocky outcrops
- ➤ Sand dunes or beaches

Each habitat will give you the chance to observe different kinds of birds. You might want to visit the sanctuary at different times of the day or year.

Hit the Trail

Most large parks have trails of various lengths that take you through different habitat areas. When you are out bird-watching, you do not need to walk or hike far—most sanctuaries have benches to sit on so you can look and listen to wildlife or enjoy a scenic view. State, national, or provincial parks usually have guides who take groups of visitors on nature walks. The guides are important bird workers, explaining what the different habitat areas are and what animals and plants are found there. These "walk and talk" hikes will help you understand the **ecology** of the area—the relationships between birds, insects, mammals, and other animals, and the plants where they live.

feathers of a wild bird. It is illegal to keep a wild bird as a pet. It is also illegal to shoot hawks, falcons, and eagles. Penalties may include huge fines of thousands of dollars and even jail time. (Native American tribes have special permits that allow them to keep eagle feathers to use for ceremonies.)

The international Migratory Bird Treaty Act was signed in 1918 to protect birds. Some species had nearly become extinct, such as the great egret, which had been killed for its long, white, fluffy plumes to be used in women's hats. Too many birds were being killed for sport: hundreds of hawks were shot each year on migration as they flew past hills and ridgetops. So a law had to be made to protect birds. (Crows, turkeys, pheasants, quail, and grouse are protected separately: each state limits the number of birds that a hunter can kill each season.)

Sanctuaries and Safe Havens

Large numbers of birds such as herons and hawks had been killed before the Migratory Bird Treaty Act was signed. To help restore the populations, the United States began setting aside large areas of habitat for birds to safely nest or migrate. In 1903, President Theodore Roosevelt ordered that

Do I Really Need Those?

If you are visiting a sanctuary or taking a guided walk led by a naturalist, you might notice that other people have brought along binoculars or field guides. Binoculars help if you are looking at birds up in a tree or very far away. Even if a bird is closer, "binocs" help to see details better. But they can be expensive and also uncomfortable to wear or carry along. If you drop them just once on a rock or pavement, they can be ruined.

However, most bird-watchers are helpful people and will gladly let you take a look through their binoculars if you are careful. At some group gatherings, there are even spotting scopes (like telescopes) set up on stands for everyone to take turns looking through.

A female eastern bluebird enters her nest box. The bluebird is the state bird of New York and Missouri.

a refuge be made for the protection of birds in Florida. Now there are more than 50 national wildlife refuges across the United States.

Each state in the United States and the provinces of Canada have sanctuaries and parks set aside as protected habitat for wildlife. They often have restrictions on human activity—some may not allow camping, campfires, or off-road vehicles.

Many do not allow dogs, even on a leash. (A study in Australia showed that fewer birds were seen on hiking trails where dogs were being walked.)

Small parks and even some public gardens are also safe havens for birds. The land is managed so that there are plenty of good nesting sites as well as trees and shrubs that produce seeds or berries. Trails or areas where birds are nesting are sometimes

Hawthorn berries are eaten by robins, cedar waxwings, and evening grosbeaks.

closed off to any human activity. There may also be several birdhouses set up for bluebirds or tree swallows.

People who have homes surrounded by fields or woodlands also like to make safe havens for birds on their property. They may keep pets indoors or in a fenced area, and they let native shrubs and food plants grow, to allow plenty of safe feeding or resting areas for birds.

Extinct Species and Conservation

Several species of birds have become extinct. Here are some examples:

- The great auk, a penguinlike bird, was hunted for food until there were none left. It became extinct around 1844.

- Millions of passenger pigeons in North America were also killed for food. By 1900, there were probably none left in the wild. The very last one, kept in captivity at the Cincinnati Zoo, died in 1914. Its name was Martha.

- The Carolina parakeet was the only native parrot in the eastern United States. It became extinct around 1920.

- The most famous extinct bird is probably the dodo, a flightless bird that lived on the island of Mauritius. The last one was killed around 1680.

Getting Organized. To try to save other birds from extinction, many different organizations work to preserve critical habitats and educate the public. The National Audubon Society was organized in 1916 to bring attention to birds and their habitats that needed protection. The Nature Conservancy was formed in 1951. And the American Bird Conservancy has many projects to create sanctuaries and promote habitat preservation. In England, the International Council for Bird Preservation was started in 1922. Several other groups have also been active in educating people about birds and the environment.

Two Important Laws. Aside from the Migratory Bird Treaty Act of 1918, there are two other laws that have been important in protecting birds and saving habitats. The Endangered Species Act of 1973 has helped to protect many species of rare birds. And in 1972 the pesticide DDT was banned by the Environmental Protection Agency. These laws are important because many species of birds around the world are still in need of protection. Here are just a few examples:

- In South America, some parrots have become rare because they are trapped and sold as pets. There are probably fewer than 1,000 Lear's macaws left. And there may be fewer than 200 Fuertes' parrots left.

- Spoonbill sandpipers, which nest in Arctic Russia, have declined sharply in number. When they migrate south, they are often trapped and sold for food. Many of the wetland habitats where they once fed have been developed for agriculture. There are now only about 200 spoonbills left.

- On the Hawaiian Islands, many species have become rare. There are only about 500 Maui parrotbills left. And the Hawaiian crow, called the alala, now survives only in captivity. There are about 60 left, and biologists hope that the birds can be bred in captivity in enough numbers to release to the wild.

Several other species have needed extraordinary efforts to preserve the current populations and protect nesting

Become a Bird Worker

Many types of trees, shrubs, and other plants provide food, shelter, or nesting sites for birds. You can adopt and care for a bird-friendly tree or shrub. It always feels great when you've done something to help birds!

Materials

Adult supervision required
- Watering can or hose
- Hedge clippers or pruning shears
- Your bird journal
- A pen or pencil

Keep an eye on any small shrub or tree to see if birds use it to rest or to get seeds or berries. If it is useful to birds, ask an adult what type of shrub it is. Many houses and schools have evergreen shrubs such as hemlock or American arborvitae planted nearby. They can be easily pruned to stay small or make a hedge.

Ask if it would be OK for you or your class to help take care of the shrub. It may need to be watered if

the weather has been very dry. It may need to have dead or broken branches trimmed away (ask for help from an adult). You might want other people to know that it is an important shrub.

Many nature centers and parks give "tree talks" similar to bird walks. If you can go on a guided tree tour, you'll learn more about the trees and shrubs in your area. In your bird journal, add information about your adopted tree or shrub and what birds you see there.

habitats: Kirtland's warblers, Atlantic puffins, least terns, Bicknell's thrushes, trumpeter swans, grasshopper sparrows, and whooping cranes—to list a few.

Good Work

Naturalists, biologists, and conservationists have created programs and projects to help save many different species from becoming extinct. One good example is the work to save the piping plover. This small shorebird nests on the Atlantic coast from Newfoundland to North Carolina and on lakeshores in the central United States. It needs a safe, sandy beach to nest and raise its young. But its habitat has decreased, and many beach areas are unsafe. People running along the beach or making fires frighten the adult plovers from settling down to incubate eggs or feed their chicks. ATV riders and loose dogs run over the nests and kill plover chicks. To prevent such disasters, local conservation groups work with towns to protect individual nests. Fences are put up around a nest site with signs asking people to avoid disturbing the area.

Conservationists have had good success with restoring peregrine falcons. The falcons were being poisoned by DDT and other pesticides, and their populations suffered a steep decline in the 1960s and 1970s. DDT had been sprayed on plants and insects, which in turn were eaten by mammals and small birds that the falcons ate. The chemicals caused the falcons' eggs to have very thin shells, so the eggs broke whenever the birds tried to sit and incubate them. Conservation organizations and universities had to set up captive-breeding programs to restore the population. Falconers helped with some of the programs,

This piping plover chick is just a few days old. The nest, chicks, and adults all need a protected, safe beach area to survive.

These peregrine chicks were part of a captive-breeding project to restore the population. When fully grown, they were released to the wild.

because they know how to tame and handle the birds. Pairs of peregrines successfully nested and laid eggs in special outdoor enclosures and were fed food that was not contaminated. Their chicks, when grown, were then released to the wild. These efforts to restore the falcons have worked, and now there is a much larger population of peregrines in the United States, Canada, and Great Britain.

Another comeback was made by bald eagles and ospreys. The osprey became rare in the United States and Great Britain by the 1970s. Many were shot, and more were killed by DDT and other poisons. Bald eagles also became rare because of chemical pesticides. After DDT was banned, the populations of both species began to rise again.

The California condor is now extremely rare. Condors had been shot by hunters and also poisoned. Today, there are as few as 200 left in the wild. Captive-breeding efforts have been somewhat successful, but much more needs to be done to ensure their survival.

Design a Poster About a Rare or Endangered Species

There may be a rare or endangered bird in your own state or province. Your school, library, or local birding club might be happy to show off a creative poster that you have made about that bird!

Materials

⬦ Scissors
⬦ Old magazines and newspapers
⬦ Crayons, colored pencils, or pens
⬦ Glue
⬦ Poster paper (or a piece of cardboard)

1. Cut words like "Save" or "Now" from newspaper or magazine advertisements.

2. Cut out colored stars, banners, or big exclamation points from the ads.

3. Look in a book or online for a photo or picture of the rare or endangered bird you'd like to show on your poster.

4. Make your own drawing of the bird, and paste it onto the poster paper.

5. Arrange the cut-out words like "Save!" around your drawing, and then paste them in place.

6. Write or draw the name of the bird in big letters (or you can cut letters out from newspaper or magazine headlines). Add on any other drawings that help show the bird's habitat or food.

Great job! Now you can hang or tape your poster in a place where people can learn about the bird—and then become interested in birds themselves!

Bird Words

Glossary

accidentals: Birds that are seen far from their natural nesting habitat or wintering areas, usually because they were blown off-course by storms.

adaptation: Developing a specialized beak, legs, feet, talons, or even wing shape. Herons have long, daggerlike beaks for fishing. A Cooper's hawk has short, rounded wings to fly fast through the forest. Adaptations are necessary for a bird to survive in its habitat.

anting: An anting bird crouches down on or near an anthill to allow the ants to crawl all over its feathers. The ants probably leave a substance called formic acid that repels feather parasites.

Aves: The class of animals that birds belong to. Birds are avians, and flight cages are called aviaries.

camouflage: Colors or patterns that make it difficult to see a bird in its natural habitat. Piping plovers have sand-colored backs and are very hard to see when they stop and settle down on the beach.

carrion: Dead or decomposing animals. Vultures feed on road-killed animals and other carrion, as do crows.

casting: A compact oval or rounded mass of fur or feathers, sometimes with bones or parts of bones, which is spit up (regurgitated) by a hawk or owl.

countershading: Having a white or light-colored underside and a darker upper body. A blue jay is mostly blue above, with a white or whitish underside.

cultivated: Describes a tree or plant that is developed, propagated, and grown from a wild species for use in gardens, landscaping, or agriculture. There are many different cultivated varieties of flowers and also fruits and vegetables—such as tomatoes. Trees can be cultivated from cuttings—when twigs are cut and rooted to start a new tree. Cultivated plants are sold at nurseries and garden centers.

cygnet: A young swan.

domesticated: Animals bred and raised to live with or work with humans, such as horses, cows, goats, and chickens. Dogs, cats, parakeets, and canaries are bred and raised as domestic pets.

ecology: The successful relationship of animals and plants living together in a habitat. A forest ecology has a different diversity of animals and plants than a desert ecology.

eyass: A young hawk, falcon, or eagle.

eye-line or eye-stripe; eye-ring: White or colored feathers that make an obvious line in front of or behind the eye; a white ring around the eye.

extinct, extinction: Not one single individual in a given species is left alive anywhere on earth. Dinosaurs are extinct. Mammoths are extinct. Passenger pigeons are extinct.

field mark: Any pattern or design that is easily noticed that helps to identify the species of a bird. The white eye-ring of an ovenbird is a good field mark. The yellow-rumped warbler is identified by its yellow rump feathers.

habitat: The natural environment that an animal needs to feed, nest, and raise its young. Thrushes usually live in a forest habitat. Red-winged blackbirds live in swampy or marshy habitats.

introduced: Describes a species that is not native to the area. Ring-necked pheasants are native to Asia, but they were introduced to North America to provide game for hunters.

keratin: A protein substance from which hair, fingernails, and feathers are made.

kettle: A group of broad-winged hawks on migration. They circle high up to take advantage of an updraft of air and then soar off.

migrate, migration, migratory: To migrate is to move to a habitat where food or nesting habitat is best. Migration usually occurs from north to south or south to north. Birds, caribou, and even some insects (such as monarch butterflies) migrate. Migratory birds move during the spring and fall.

molting: The normal shedding of feathers. New feathers grow in.

native species: A wild animal (or plant) that normally lives or grows in a particular area. The white-throated sparrow is native to most of the United States and Canada. The English sparrow (house sparrow) is native to England and Europe but was introduced to North America and is now widespread.

nonnative: Usually an introduced animal or plant. The starling is not native to North America; it was brought over from England and Europe. The dandelion is a nonnative plant; it also is native to England and Europe.

ornithologist: A scientist who studies birds.

primaries: The feathers on the leading edge of the wing. There are usually 9 or 10 primaries.

protective coloration: Colors, patterns, or countershading that help conceal a bird in its normal habitat.

rehabilitator: A person who has federal and state permits to take care of, raise, or keep injured wild animals, including birds.

resident: A species that does not usually migrate. A black-capped chickadee is a resident species, because it remains near its nesting territory all year.

scavenger: An animal that feeds on whatever it can find—insects, frogs, berries, and carrion. Crows are scavengers. Vultures scavenge for carrion.

secondaries: The smaller flight feathers on the wing, following the primaries. The secondaries are closer to the body.

species: One type of animal or plant; the birds of one species look alike in shape, structure, camouflage, color, or patterns, and they all need the same habitat for nesting; they all sing the same, act the same, and feed the same way; they don't breed with other species. A barn swallow is a separate species from a tree swallow, even though they seem quite similar.

territory: A nesting or roosting area that is defended against other birds. A nesting territory is usually "announced" by the male singing and chasing off other males of the same species.

thermal: A large, rising column of air, usually near a valley or ridge, that migrating hawks and falcons use to gain height and then easily soar away without much effort.

tiercel: A male falcon. Tiers is a French word meaning one-third. Many male falcons and hawks are nearly one-third smaller than females.

tundra: A treeless arctic habitat.

ultraviolet (UV) light: A color of light that humans cannot see but some birds can.

wing bar: A white or light-colored line or bar across the upper part of the wing. A bird may have one or two wing bars, and these are good field marks.

Bird Orders

Birds belong to the class Aves. Order, listed below, is a subset of class, and family is a subset of order. After each order, a few examples from the families are given. Some orders just have one family; others have many. Within each family, there are further divisions: genera (plural for genus) and species.

Orders are always listed in evolutionary order, with many of the waterbirds first and the most recently evolved birds (Passeriformes) at the end.

ORDER	EXAMPLES FROM SOME OF THE FAMILIES
Gaviiformes	loons
Podicipediformes	grebes
Procellariiformes	Albatrosses, shearwaters, petrels
Pelecaniformes	pelicans, cormorants, gannets
Ciconiiformes	herons, bitterns, ibises, storks
Phoenicopteriformes	flamingos
Anseriformes	ducks, swans, geese
Falconiformes	vultures, condors, hawks, eagles, falcons
Galliformes	pheasants, grouse, turkeys, quail
Gruiformes	rails, coots, gallinules, cranes
Charadriiformes	plovers, sandpipers, gulls, terns
Columbiformes	pigeons, doves
Psittaciformes	parrots
Cuculiformes	cuckoos, roadrunners, turacos

ORDER	EXAMPLES FROM SOME OF THE FAMILIES
Strigiformes	owls
Caprimulgiformes	whip-poor-wills, nighthawks
Apodiformes	swifts, hummingbirds
Trogoniformes	trogons
Coraciiformes	kingfishers
Piciformes	woodpeckers
Passeriformes	flycatchers, swallows, jays, crows, nuthatches, wrens, warblers, bluebirds, thrushes, waxwings, starlings, vireos, finches, sparrows—and many others!

The ovenbird is a member of the Order Passeriformes.

Common and Scientific Names

Listed here are the common names of some of the birds shown in the photographs or drawings in this book, along with their scientific names. Scientific names are usually based on Latin or Greek words, with some words referring to geographic areas or the names of naturalists. Scientific names for animals and plants are always written in italics. The common names are in alphabetical order, to make it easier for you to find them.

COMMON NAME	SCIENTIFIC NAME
American black duck	*Anas rubripes*
American goldfinch	*Carduelis tristis*
American kestrel	*Falco sparverius*
American robin	*Turdus migratorius*
Baltimore oriole (northern oriole)	*Icterus galbula*
barn swallow	*Hirundo rustica*
barred owl	*Strix varia*
black-bellied plover	*Pluvialis squatarola*
brown thrasher	*Toxostoma rufum*
Canada warbler	*Wilsonia canadensis*
cedar waxwing	*Bombycilla cedrorum*
chicken	*Gallus gallus*
chipping sparrow	*Spizella passerina*

COMMON NAME	SCIENTIFIC NAME
cliff swallow	*Petrochelidon pyrrhonota*
cockatiel (Quarrion)	*Nymphicus hollandicus*
common goldeneye	*Bucephala clangula*
downy woodpecker	*Picoides pubescens*
eastern bluebird	*Sialia sialis*
eastern phoebe	*Sayornis phoebe*
emu	*Dromaius novaehollandiae*
English (house) sparrow	*Passer domesticus*
grasshopper sparrow	*Ammodramus savannarum*
great blue heron	*Ardea herodias*
great egret (American egret)	*Ardea alba*
great horned owl	*Bubo virginianus*
hairy woodpecker	*Picoides villosus*
Livingstone's turaco	*Tauraco livingstonii*
northern cardinal	*Cardinalis cardinalis*
northern goshawk	*Accipiter gentilis*
northern mockingbird	*Mimus polyglottos*
northern saw-whet owl	*Aegolius acadicus*
osprey	*Pandion haliaetus*

COMMON NAME	SCIENTIFIC NAME
ovenbird	*Seiurus aurocapillus*
parakeet (budgerigar)	*Melopsittacus undulatus*
peacock (common peafowl)	*Pavo cristatus*
peregrine falcon	*Falco peregrinus*
pigeon (rock dove; carrier pigeon)	*Columba livia*
pileated woodpecker	*Dryocopus pileatus*
piping plover	*Charadrius melodus*
prairie warbler	*Dendroica discolor*
purple gallinule	*Porphyrio martinica*
red-breasted nuthatch	*Sitta canadensis*
red-winged blackbird	*Agelaius phoeniceus*
resplendent quetzal	*Pharomachrus mocinno*
ring-billed gull	*Larus delawarensis*
ruby-throated hummingbird	*Archilochus colubris*
ruddy turnstone	*Arenaria interpres*
ruffed grouse	*Bonasa umbellus*
snowy owl	*Nyctea scandiaca*
wild turkey	*Meleagris gallopavo*
yellow warbler	*Dendroica petechia*

Resources

There are many organizations with online information about birds and other wildlife. Here are just a few that teachers and students may find interesting. Just type in the name of the organization, or the website address.

Cornell Lab of Ornithology (the Lab manages Project FeederWatch, NestWatch and other "citizen science" programs): www.birds.cornell.edu

Fundación ProAves: www.proaves.org (English and Spanish)

Hawk Mountain Sanctuary: www.hawkmountain.org

HawkWatch International: www.hawkwatch.org

International Migratory Bird Day: www.birdday.org

Nature Canada: www.naturecanada.ca

Nature Conservancy: www.nature.org

Partners in Flight: www.partnersinflight.com

Raptor Research Foundation: www.raptorresearchfoundation.org

Royal Society for the Protection of Birds (England): www.rspb.org.uk

Also look for local information by searching by the name of a state, province, or city organization, such as Mass Audubon Society, Montana Audubon, or Golden Gate Raptor Observatory.

Teacher's Guide

Here are some topics and activities for classroom or independent study.

- Put together a "bird word" spelling bee

- Write a bird poem—it can be a funny one!

- Design a poster about your state or provincial bird

- Find out if there are any rare or endangered species in your area

- Write a report about your favorite bird

- Discuss what these sayings mean:

  - *Eyes like a hawk.*
  - *Wise as an owl.*
  - *Birds of a feather flock together.*
  - *A bird's-eye view.*
  - *In the catbird seat.*

- Discuss a special habitat in your area

- Make a bird word scramble or a multiple choice guessing game

- Discuss world environmental issues:

  - *There are only about 200 spoonbill sandpipers left in Arctic Russia and about 200 California condors remaining in the wild, while there are at least 20,000 polar bears left. Why do you think that the bears get all the urgent attention?*

  - *Why should biologists and ornithologists care about birds in distant countries?*

  - *How will climate change affect the population of birds? What about the insects or seeds they eat?*

- Learn about two avian heroes of World War I: the carrier pigeon Cher Ami and the Pigeon of Verdun. Both birds had missions to carry important messages.

- Find out about some famous names in ornithology:

  - *John James Audubon (1785–1851)*
  - *Thomas Bewick (1753–1828)*
  - *Elliott Coues (1842–99)*
  - *Louis Agassiz Fuertes (1874–1927)*
  - *Roger Tory Peterson (1908–96)*
  - *Alexander Wilson (1766–1813)*

- Learn about the birds the ancient Egyptians used in art and as hieroglyphs, icons, and symbols, such as:

  - *Horus the falcon, a sun god*
  - *Thoth, the ibis, who represented the wisdom of scribes*
  - *The swallow, a form taken at night by the mythical goddess Isis*

Three avian symbols in the art of ancient Egypt: (*left to right*) Horus the falcon; Thoth the ibis; and the swallow.

- *Investigate the resplendent quetzal, a bird of Mexico and Central America idolized by the Aztecs and Maya hundreds of years ago. The quetzal is used today as an icon and emblem of Guatemala.*

This design of a resplendent quetzal is based on ancient Mexican and Mayan paintings and drawings.

- **Please Note: Just as there are people who are terrified of dogs or snakes, you may have a student who has a significant fear of birds. This student can accomplish other important projects that focus on habitat, such as:**

  - *Making a report about a local or state wildlife park.*
  - *Writing about a common (or rare!) tree species.*
  - *Collecting, pressing, and identifying leaves from local trees.*
  - *Designing a poster about the state tree or wildflower.*
  - *Reporting on a book or movie about the environment.*

Bibliography

Denotes titles suitable for young readers.

American Poultry Association. *Standard of Perfection.* Chicago: 39th annual meeting publication of the APA, 1915.

Austin, Oliver L. Jr. *Families of Birds.* New York: Golden Press / Western Publishing Co., 1971.

Bent, Arthur Cleveland. *Life Histories of North American Cardinals, Grosbeaks, Buntings, Towhees, Finches, Sparrows and Allies.* Parts One, Two, and Three. New York, NY: Dover Publications, Inc., 1968.

Bent, Arthur Cleveland. *Life Histories of North American Wood Warblers.* Parts One and Two. New York: Dover Publications, Inc., 1963.

Burrows, Roger. *Birding in Atlantic Canada: Volume 2: Newfoundland.* St. John's, Newfoundland: Jesperson Press, Ltd., 1989.

Coues, Elliott. *Key to North American Birds.* 4th ed. Boston: Estes and Lauriat, 1896.

Davis, L. Irby. *A Field Guide to the Birds of Mexico and Central America.* Austin, TX: University of Texas Press, 1972.

Durango, Sigfrid. *Faglarna i Farg [Birds in Color].* Stockholm, Sweden: Almqvist and Wiksell Forlag, 1952.

Fisk, Erma J. *The Bird with the Silver Bracelet.* South Orleans, MA: Arey's Pond Press, 1986.

Gabrielson, Ira N., and Frederick C. Lincoln. *Birds of Alaska.* Harrisburg, PA: Stackpole Co. / Washington, DC: Wildlife Management Institute, 1959.

Harrison, Colin, and Alan Greensmith. *Birds of the World.* New York: Dorling Kindersley, 1993.

Harrison, Hal H. *A Field Guide to Birds' Nests in the United States East of the Mississippi River.* Boston: Houghton Mifflin Co., 1975.

Heinzel, Hermann, Richard Fitter, and John Parslow. *The Birds of Britain and Europe.* London: Wm. Collins and Sons, Co. Ltd., 1977.

Hickey, Joseph J., ed. *Peregrine Falcon Populations: Their Biology and Decline.* Madison, WI: University of Wisconsin Press, 1969.

Hill, Geoffrey E. *National Geographic Bird Coloration.* Washington, DC: National Geographic Society, 2010.

Kaufmann, John, and Heinz Meng. *Falcons Return: Restoring an Endangered Species*. 2nd ed. Unionville, NY: KAV Books, 1992.

Kortright, Francis H. *The Ducks, Geese and Swans of North America*. Harrisburg, PA: Stackpole Co. / Washington, DC: Wildlife Management Institute, 1953.

Kress, Stephen W. *Bird Life*. New York: St. Martin's Press, 1991.

Lanyon, Wesley E. *Biology of Birds*. Garden City, NY: The Natural History Press / American Museum of Natural History, 1963.

Lawson, Don. *The United States in World War I*. New York: Scholastic Magazines, Inc., 1964.

Lincoln, Frederick C. *Migration of Birds*. Circular 16. Washington, DC: US Department of the Interior / Fish and Wildlife Service, 1950.

Martin, Alexander C., Herbert S. Zim, and Arnold L. Neslon. *American Wildlife and Plants: A Guide to Wildlife Food Habits*. New York: Dover Publications, Inc., 1961.

McCollough, Mark, et al. *Maine's Endangered and Threatened Wildlife*. Augusta, ME: Maine Dept. of Inland Fisheries and Wildlife, 2003.

Mountfort, Guy. *Rare Birds of the World: A Collins/ICBP Handbook*. Lexington, MA: Stephen Green Press, Inc. / Penguin Group, 1988.

Nuttall, Zelia, ed. *The Codex Nuttall*. New York: Dover Publications, 1975.

Patrick, Richard. *All Color Book of Egyptian Mythology*. London: Octopus Books Ltd., 1972.

* Peterson, Roger Tory. *A Field Guide to the Birds East of the Rockies*. Boston: Houghton Mifflin Co., 1980.

Pettingill, Olin Sewall Jr. *Ornithology in Laboratory and Field*. 4th ed. Minneapolis, MN: Burgess Publishing Co., 1970.

Pizzey, Graham. *A Field Guide to the Birds of Australia*. Princeton, NJ: Princeton University Press, 1994.

* Robbins, Chandler S., Bertel Bruun, and Herbert S. Zim. *Birds of North America*. New York: Golden Press / Western Publishing Co., 1983.

Shipman, Pat. *Taking Wing: Archaeopteryx and the Evolution of Bird Flight*. London: Phoenix/Orion Books Ltd., 1999.

* Sibley, David Allen. *The Sibley Field Guide to Birds of Eastern North America*. New York: Alfred A. Knopf, 2003.

* Sterry, Paul, and Brian E. Small. *Birds of Eastern North America: A Photographic Guide*. Princeton, NJ, and Oxfordshire, UK: Princeton University Press, 2009.

Terres, John K. *Songbirds in Your Garden*. New York: Thomas Crowell Co., 1968.

Vriends, Matthew M. *Simon and Schuster's Guide to Pet Birds*. New York: Simon and Schuster, 1984.

Walls, Gordon Lynn. *The Vertebrate Eye*. Bloomfield Hills, MI: Cranbrook Institute of Science, 1942.

Other Resources

Many monographs, newspaper articles, magazine articles, and reports were studied and considered to complete this book—even the mention of birds in radio and television programs. Here are some examples: *Living Bird* magazine, *Living Bird News*, *BirdScope*, and other reports from Cornell's Lab of Ornithology; the American Bird Conservancy's *Bird Calls* reports and *Bird Conservation* magazine; *Nature Conservancy* magazine; online information about the Dickin Medal from www.pdsa.org.uk; *Audubon* magazine; and *Bird Watcher's Digest* magazine.

Leaflets and trail maps from local and state parks and trail systems were also helpful, as were several documentary movies about the environment, bird migration, and Antarctic wildlife.

Index